Inner PEACE Outer ABUNDANCE

Latonia King
May you both continue
to experience
inner peace &
outer abundance

Kim Hà Campbell

Kim Hà Campbell

Inner PEACE Outer ABUNDANCE

ISBN-13: 978-1523241873

Inner PEACE Outer ABUNDANCE

Table Of Contents

Introduction

"Peace and Abundance is our birthright" – Kim Ha Campbell

In the past, if you had asked me if I'd ever write a book, I would have answered with a big, fat, "NO! Are you crazy?" Although I communicate well in person, writing is especially challenging for me since English is not my first language. The thought of becoming a published author had never crossed my mind. Besides, my story is not quite done yet, so why write it now? Then again, sometimes I wonder if I'm ever going to be done. I'm only getting started. I'm a semi-finished product, and I still have much room to grow. But I know in my heart, based on the transformational stories that happened for the many clients I've been coaching, I think this is selfish of me not to at least share my journey with you. I don't have a destination; I'm simply enjoying and loving the adventure of my life. I do have lots of creative goals, and you will see more of me sooner than later. I just know that, as long as I am having fun I am on the right journey. Throughout my journey, I learned that, many times, we were on a path, and then God has a different plan for us, and it's okay. The goal is to have fun, stay open, adapt, listen, and always do what's best for us. Here is how the book came about.

People have been seeking me out for years now, asking for advice, and I would share my true-life experiences with anyone. My life has been filled with obstacles, yet I've found ways to overcome them and continue moving forward. I knew that my story could inspire people to become more and follow their heart's deepest desires.

It seems the more I share my story, the more people get inspired. The results amaze me because I don't look at myself as anyone special. These powerful lessons were ready to have a life of their own.

In July 2011, I had achieved a certain level of success in my business and was invited to speak to a women's empowerment group of over 1,500 ladies. There I was, this accomplished woman who had escaped the horrors of war, overcome stereotypes, and survived abuse and bad relationships – and I was totally freaking out! They had positioned me as a speaker?! Who the heck am I to tell these women anything?

My nerves climbed from a 3 to 100. As the event continued on, it was clear that they were running over time and I hadn't even been on stage yet. My nerves came back down as I crumpled my notes and let out a deep sigh of relief... they'd have to reschedule me.

Then out of nowhere, the Master of Ceremonies announced my name!

I went out on this huge stage without any notes and stood in front of all of those women. I did the only thing I could. I went straight to my heart and knew that God would speak through me.

As I began telling my story, I saw faces of concern and worry in the crowd. I saw some women crying and reaching for tissues. When I finished, the response was overwhelming. Every woman in the audience was on her feet, cheering loudly. I got to see, firsthand, how we could inspire others if we have the courage to share our stories and be our true, authentic selves. That experience was the first time I shared the philosophy for my life; I call it "Inner Peace Outer Abundance."

So what is Inner Peace Outer Abundance?

Looking back, I realize that I always wanted Inner Peace and Outer Abundance at the same time, but everyone around me was saying I had to settle for one or the other. I started to question why no one seemed to believe that both could coexist.

There is not a cookie cutter definition of Inner Peace, Outer Abundance. This is not a "One size fits all" concept. It is different for everyone since we are each unique beings with our own set of DNA, influences, and environmental experiences.

I can tell you, it is a way of life. It is living out the full expression of your authentic self to reach your heart's desire. That is why, for me, I always refer to it as one concept- Inner Peace Outer Abundance. It manifests itself physically, spiritually, and financially. What I have learned is that, without Inner Peace Outer Abundance, our true selves are being hidden from the world and will be buried with us in our graves. Ultimately you will have to define it for yourself as you go on this adventurous journey with me. Very few people achieve Inner Peace Outer Abundance, but, because you are holding this book, you might be one of the lucky ones.

This book is my journey. The purpose of this book is NOT to sell you anything; I'm not selling a product, a service, or using my story as a way to make money. I am going to share with you a powerful system that continues to bless me, and I hope it will bless you too. Perhaps it can inspire you to no longer choose to live in a world where judgment, fear, comparison and other people's opinion guide your decisions and choices. You can learn to listen to that inner voice, inner guidance, or gut feeling. For me, it's what I call my inner child. The desires of your heart will become your compass, and peace and abundance is your endless path. I believe inner peace outer abundance is our birthright.

I came from nothing. I was a war refugee without a home and living in a strange land. I barely even spoke the language. In spite of these challenges, I made the choice to take advantage of every opportunity that presented itself. I learned so much along the way and I'm excited to share my hard-earned wisdom and insights with you so that, you can have it all too. I want you to know that no matter where you are today, when you find out how to overcome anything by having peace, love, and abundance, you will be blessed beyond measure.

My journey gave birth to my BEACH Success System, which I use to coach thousands of people around the world to find their Inner Peace Outer Abundance. It has positively impacted so many people spiritually, emotionally, and financially, and it can do the same for you. I trust you will enjoy reading this book because my life was not perfect and I don't sugarcoat anything.

Oh, and to those people that have been asking me to write my story... here it is!

Chapter 1

Voyage to Freedom

"It's in the moments of decision your destiny is shaped."

– Anthony Robbins

After North Vietnam took over South Vietnam in 1975, my family had a plan for my brothers to escape from our country; that was the thing to do. Most of the other families were doing it, but the girls were never in the plan...never. It was considered to be too dangerous.

For starters, there was only a 50 percent chance of surviving the ocean voyage to freedom. My mother told me hundreds of times, "Any girl caught trying to escape was sent to prison where you were raped and subjected to horrible and unimaginable tortures. If pirates got hold of you, it was even worse. They would make you a slave." This was why girls were not included in the plan to escape from my country.

I walked into my house on an otherwise ordinary night when I was 13 years old. You can imagine what an unexpected event it was for me when I was just being my normal, happy-go-lucky-self only to find my sister, mother, and father crying and sobbing in our living room.

An instantaneous grief hits you when you walk into a room where the patriarch of your family is crying. I didn't know how to feel, but as soon as my mother saw me, a shining light of hope and vision burst from her eyes.

She opened her arms for me to come sit on her lap. Of course, I ran and jumped into the comfort of my mother's embrace. I wanted to cry and I didn't know why.

My mother wiped away her tears and looked at me with the deepest expression of care before saying "My beautiful little flower, if there was a chance for you to escape from Vietnam tonight, would you do it?"

I was stunned. The only word I could manage was "what?" My mind was racing: I don't know how to swim! What about the sharks and the pirates? They scared us with stories about sharks and pirates all the time in hopes that we would never consider escaping. Finally, I managed, "After all those warnings about sharks and pirates, now you want me to go? Are you kidding me?"

My father was more serious than I had ever seen him in my life, "Yes, it's scary, but you don't have much of a future here in Vietnam." I reacted, "But you said we could never escape. Not girls!" I was wondering if this was a trick question! I had never experienced that sort of tension in our home before.

I knew that my sister was going, but she had no choice; she was married so it was her husband's choice. As for me, there was no way they would choose for me to do this. Would they?

Emotions raced through my 13-year-old body, mind, and spirit. I was scared, yet at the same time I was excited, thinking I had the shot I thought I would never ever have in Vietnam...ever!

As far as I knew, my parents never talked about escaping illegally. I had been told that if we were to ever leave it would be in a legal way. We would fly away from the country on a plane, or because someone sponsored us so we could come to their country. My parents had been trying for years, but none of us had any real hope of ever getting out of Vietnam through legal channels.

I sat in silence as I thought about myself, my life, and my future. My dad was right; I didn't have a shot at any kind of successful life in Vietnam. I had already quit school and was helping my parents run a little restaurant. As far as I could tell, I would be running that little restaurant for the rest of my life.

I never wanted to run a restaurant; I did it because they needed help and I was the only child left in the house. All of their other children were married or had already escaped from the country.

Fleeting images of a better future raced through my head as the sorrow of leaving my parents washed over my heart. Wracked with conflicting emotions, I stammered, "B-b-but who's going to take care of everything? Who's going to take care of you guys if I go?" At that moment, the thought of leaving them felt wrong, as if I was abandoning them.

My mom grasped me firmly but lovingly by both shoulders, looked deep into my eyes, straight through my soul, and into our future. "If you go, you can help us later." I slowly pulled away from her and she released me with a sad smile. I needed a moment to think, to realize that this was really happening, and that they were waiting on my decision. My mother's words summoned a courage from somewhere deep inside of me that I didn't know existed. I couldn't imagine a new life without them. I didn't know how I could leave them, especially my mom.

As if reading my mind, my dad said, "Don't worry. I will take care of your mother. If you go and the plan works out, one day you can save us all."

Trusting in them, and believing there was a bigger purpose for my life, I softly said, in almost a whisper, "Alright. When do we leave?"

After an emotional time of crying, hugging, and kissing my father and mother goodbye, my sister grabbed me by the hand and led me briskly toward the front door. I did not have the chance to pack anything as there was no time. All I took with me were the clothes I was wearing. Little did I know I would never see my father alive again.

"Do you think we should grab some food?" I asked her. "Don't talk. Don't talk about anything. No time right now. We're late. We've got to go now." That was the entire conversation. We jumped into a pedicab, and my sister instructed the driver to hurry as fast as he could across our tiny town. Today, Soc Trang is a big city, but in 1986, it was so small that when you went to the market, you knew everybody.

As I looked over the side of the whizzing pedicab, streets and houses and markets flashed before my eyes. In the memory of my 13-year-old self, it seemed like we were almost instantly on the muddy banks of the Cau Quay River. It was pitch dark and I could see people moving around, but I couldn't see who they were or what they were doing. All I could put together was that people were walking on and off wobbly planks laid out across the mud, stretching all the way out to a boat in the deep water.

My sister paid the driver before dragging me by the hand over to a man in long, dark pants and a dark long-sleeve shirt. I was surprised that I recognized him. He had been hanging out at our house for the past few days. It was by no means unusual for strangers to stay at my parent's house, because people would come from all over Vietnam and stay with us from time to time. My mom welcomed people into our home; that's the kind of woman she was her whole life. I quickly gathered that this man who'd been staying at our house for the past two days was actually the captain of the boat on which we were escaping. My sister told the captain, "Just me and my baby sister. My husband's not coming."

He nodded and put two check marks on his list, then we quickly scampered onto the wobbly wooden planks across the mud and all the way out to the boat. In the deep water, it was quiet except for the sounds of the river splashing against the hull. I couldn't hear any talking or noise coming from the boat, even though I could make out crowds of people silhouetted on the deck.

This was a cargo ship, built completely of wood, and designed to carry four crew members and cargo, yet it was crowded with 215 people. All 45 feet of it sat deep in the water under the weight of overloaded human cargo.

A strong pair of hands grabbed me by my shoulders and literally tossed me over the rail and onto the boat. I was startled as I landed on my backside with a hard thud. As I looked around, nobody spoke. No questions. No chit-chat. Nothing. Just nervous eyes looking at me or scanning the banks of the river for any signs of trouble. Seemingly out of nowhere, a sailor scooped me up and tossed me down an opening into the belly of the boat. I was all alone and I had no idea what happened to my sister.

Inside, it smelled like mud, diesel fuel, and sweat. The heat and humidity were almost unbearable. You could sense the tension inside the boat and see fear in everyone's eyes. Everyone was terrified at the idea of not surviving. It was a "doomed" kind of terror. I imagine it must have been a similar feeling for the people waiting to enter the gas chamber at a Nazi concentration camp. I thought to myself, *this is it. We're about to cross the point of no return. We don't know what's going to happen. What's going to become of us?*

Being so tiny, I was able to scramble into a corner next to a small boy. I hugged my bare legs as I whimpered on the floor. The boy and I were both scared and crying. I didn't know where my sister was or even if she had made it onto the boat. I felt all alone even though we were packed into that boat like sardines.

I turned to investigate why there was water on my arms only to find I wasn't the only one crying; soft sobs were coming from the boy sitting next to me in the corner. I cried and cried and cried until I fell asleep. A few hours later I was awakened by motion and the rocking of the boat. I stood on my tiptoes and looked out a tiny porthole to see that we were moving down the river. It was dark and terrifying. All I could see was water. It was very late, and everyone was asleep, so I sat down again beside the little boy, hugging myself until consumed by the sweet oblivion of sleep.

I woke to the sound of the captain's voice yelling, and soon all the crew was echoing him. Then there was a terrified murmur throughout the passengers, "Pirates!"

Suddenly, the captain craned his neck down from the deck, and looked in through a large cargo hole above me. As he scanned the frightened faces, his eyes suddenly seized on mine, "You, girl. Your mom told me to take care of her family, so I'll take care of you. Do as I say, and put coal on your face fast, because if they catch you they're going to rape you and they're going to kill you."

Curiosity got the better of me. Once I had my face blackened with coal, I climbed up a ladder and went onto the deck of the ship. The captain looked me over and nodded at my dirty disguise before pointing at a small boat about 100 meters behind us. I could see men wearing black and red clothing and holding guns.

Pirates!

Thick billows of smoke rose off the back of our boat as the engines churned at full speed in attempt to evade the pirate boat. Even at the pace we were going, their little ship seemed to be getting closer and closer; more and more details of the red and black t-shirts and bandannas tied around their faces becoming more visible every second.

Eventually, we got up enough speed to outrun them. The pirate ship soon fell still in the water and became smaller and smaller on the horizon before slowly becoming a tiny dot with a trail of smoke rising up into the blue sky. Then the smoke trailed off and the boat disappeared.

There had been talk among the passengers that there was no way our little cargo boat could possibly make it across such a huge ocean. Everyone knew it. So being rescued had always been part of the plan.

Just before sunset, we saw a big boat that looked like a freighter. The captain steered us closer. This boat could possibly take us all on as "political refugees" and save us. However, as we neared the big freighter, it soon became clear that this was a Russian boat, which was very bad. "If the Russians get you, where do you think you are going to end up? Back home. The Russians are Communists." So, we turned away from the Russian boat, and chugged slowly into the darkness of the endlessly open sea.

The next day we struck oil — literally! As I sat on the deck of the ship squinting into the morning sun, off in the distance was a tiny dot on the horizon. As we moved toward the dot, it rose up higher and higher above the sea, and as we came closer, that dot became a platform standing high in the air above the ocean. It was an oil drilling platform run by British Petroleum.

When we got next to the platform, the captain and a translator climbed up a ladder onto a boat sent out by the rig to intercept us and everyone came up on deck to watch. My sister and I were reunited by this time, and we stood there hugging. We were both still smudged with coal, but our eyes shone brightly as we looked hopefully towards the oil platform. We all knew that, if they would take us, this would be our salvation.

Next thing we knew, the captain was shouting instructions down to his crew and soon we were all climbing up a ladder to the oil platform. It was a very long way to pull myself up on the hard, slippery steel rungs. At the time, it seemed to go on forever and my little arms and hand muscles were tired when I finally was hoisted the last few rungs onto the platform by an Englishman in a dirty white tank-top shirt.

When everyone was off the boat, the BP crew lined us up near the edge of the platform and hosed us down with water from a fire hose. While we were all being rinsed, I watched a small boat from the oil platform tow our old wooden ship away. Then there was an explosion that ripped a huge hole in the bow of the cargo boat and sent it to its final resting place beneath the sea. Sitting on the edge of the oil platform, eating bowls of Ramen noodles, we watched our old boat fade away beneath the ocean. There were so many people on the fishing boat that the main concern had been water and diesel fuel, so all they had fed us was porridge for two days. Ramen noodles never tasted so great!

As my belly filled, and smoke from the sinking boat dissipated into the air, I felt an overwhelming sense of peace. Wow, it's real! I escaped death. Most people who tried to escape Vietnam were never heard from again. Most died. Everybody was relieved and happy to be there on the oil platform. We survived floating on the ocean for three long days. We had officially escaped Vietnam!

This was the first time I breathed the fresh air of freedom.

Chapter 2

Apple and 7 Up

"The starting point of all achievement is desire. Keep this constantly in mind." –Napoleon Hill

---

The day after we boarded the oil rig, they took us to Kuku Island, Indonesia. This was a tent village filled with 2,000 short-term refugees like us. They were mostly Vietnamese and had also survived treacherous ocean voyages. It didn't hit me until we arrived to the island that we would no longer be able to see our Mom and Dad. Growing up, I was extremely attached to my parents, especially the nurturing of my mother. The realization that I was no longer going to see them anymore shocked my whole being. I was so upset- crying uncontrollably and throwing up. As a 13-year-old girl, I just did not have the maturity to comprehend the enormity of what had just happened. I was continuously thinking of my parents; we had no communication with them. I was wondering, *are they worrying about me?*

From Kuku Island, they quickly transitioned us to the Galang Refugee Camp where they put us all into long, tin-roof barracks. My sister and I shared the corner space of our barracks with a man and his son, who was my age. That corner of the barracks was home for the first year we lived at Galang One. Other refugees from all over Vietnam were also warehoused at Galang. Many of them had been there five to ten years, waiting to be sponsored by another nation: Australia, America, Canada,

Holland, any country willing to be a sponsor. Everyone at Galang was playing the waiting game; get sponsored or be sent back to Vietnam.

I wouldn't really call it living; it's actually just surviving while waiting for sponsorship paperwork. We were waiting to see if our brothers could be our sponsors. An official worker at the camp took my picture and asked what I was doing on the oil platform. My sister had coached me to say, "I'm from Vietnam; I'm escaping as a political refugee."

Paperwork is everything for refugees; it's their only focus, their only hope. It begins on day one when they photograph all the refugees and give them a piece of paper equivalent to an ID. From then on, whenever the refugees spoke, they had to reference their ID and the boat number from the boat in which they traveled. They called this your "cycle." Ours was "Cycle 89." Whenever anyone referred to "Cycle 89," everyone on our boat listened hopefully for the announcement. There were probably about 215 people in "Cycle 89," completely made up of survivors from our boat. I was so grateful that I had made it this far! Although, being in a refugee camp was not part of the plan.

The funny thing is, I was not in "the plan" in many ways. I wasn't even supposed to be born. I was an accident! Seriously. My mom always laughed when she spoke of me as a baby because my last brother was born in 1968 and my mother had said, "After 10 kids, no more!" She was on birth control, but then four years later she was pregnant and wondered, "What am I going to do?"

She went to the nurse to get an injection to get rid of the baby, but without her knowing, the nurse gave her vitamins to keep the baby healthy. She wondered, "Oh my God! Why am I still getting bigger?" By then it was too late, and she could no longer do anything about it, so my mother and father resigned themselves: "All right, one more baby. But this is it."

They weren't looking forward to a new, unplanned baby until I was born. My being a girl was a Godsend! My mom was thrilled to have another girl. She only had two daughters and the rest were boys. You can imagine how hard it was for my mother to send her baby girl across the ocean.

As much as I was grateful to have been rescued, and have a brighter future, life at the refugee camp was pretty harsh. I had left a great life in Vietnam and it was depressing to have no money and no comfort. Although, in a way, I actually had more freedom in the refugee camp than in Vietnam. My inner child had more freedom to play, and I even got to be a Girl Scout. This was the beginning of noticing the contrast of having money but no time, or having lots of time and no money.

Back home, I had the money but no time. I dropped out of school at the age of 11, and had been running the family's restaurant since then. That was going to be my entire future unless, or until, I got married and moved away with my husband. All my brothers and sisters had already gotten married and moved out, so, as the last remaining child at home, I ran the family restaurant like a little pint-sized entrepreneur, doing just about everything to support my mom and dad.

We were famous for a noodle dish called Bun Nem Nuong; it's a popular dish of noodles and Vietnamese meatballs. The meatballs are very basic, made of pork with garlic, salt, and sugar. It has a special flavor because we mix the meat together with pork fat, which makes it very tasty. To make the dish, we separated the pork fat from the meat, then chopped the pork fat into smaller pieces, and then caramelized it with sugar in a big mixing bowl, which made the fat crispy. We ground the pork meat with the herbs and other ingredients until it was chewy. Then we mixed the crispy caramelized fat into the pulverized meat, and rounded it out into little balls, which we put on chopsticks and grilled over hot coals.

From the time I was 11, I made hundreds of those meatballs from scratch every day. I woke up every morning around 5 o'clock, sometimes by will, and many times by my father whipping me with a black hose from the tire pump. That's why I hate spankings. My mom never spanked me, ever. She was all love and would use words to discipline us, telling us how we could improve our behavior.

It's funny how my dad used loving force and my mom used loving words. I loved my dad and respected him, and I know he only did what he had to do, but I was most endeared with my mom's technique.

Every morning, I got up and went shopping to buy food for the family restaurant, and the two pigs I was raising. When the pigs got old enough, we would sell them for extra money. I would also buy the day's supplies for the restaurant and the family. Still rubbing the sleep from my little brown eyes, I would shuffle down the dirt road to a local market with my tiny cloth purse filled with the previous day's earnings from the restaurant. I bought fresh pork, noodles, and vegetables to go along with the ingredients for the meatballs, and then brought it all home.

The name of the restaurant is Bay Ganh. That's my dad's name. He was very well loved and well known. My family continues to run that restaurant in Vietnam to this day, and they are famous for that meatball dish throughout the country. When people hear Bay Ganh, they know the restaurant has the best recipe and they serve the best meatballs and noodles in the country.

The restaurant isn't anything fancy. We had a house and most of the family slept upstairs; downstairs was the restaurant along with the room in which my Mother, my Father, and I slept. The pigs were in the backyard.

We began serving people at about 9 o'clock in the morning. People came in all day long until we closed the shop about 10 p.m., after which we cleaned until about 11.

My dad usually locked the door. I was supposed to go to bed. But I was the kind of kid who would climb over the gate and try to get a buddy to play badminton, often until midnight. This explains why I sometimes had difficulty waking up early on my own.

Life in a refugee camp was very different. Here, you always have time. On a typical day in the barracks, somebody woke up and started moving around by about 6 or 7 in the morning, and their noise woke everybody. The camp o fficials would set up a place to get food outside of our barracks, so my sister and I would fetch our small portions of food in the mornings. It usually consisted of fish, flour, beans, and eggs. There was a community kitchen; once a week my sister and I, along with other women and girls, would go prepare food.

We felt lucky because we lived on a corner of the barracks, so it was cooler than the rest of the building. We had a jar to collect rainwater off the edge of the roof. One morning I woke up so thirsty that I grabbed a cup, without looking, and took a big gulp. It tasted horrible. I looked into the jar of rainwater, only to see that there were two dead rats in the bottom of the jar!

I tell people, "If you want to know why I'm so grateful, this is why - when you can survive with little to no food and no worldly possessions for an extended period of time, you are sure to be thankful when you do have something."

One afternoon in particular stands out in my memory in terms of gratitude. There was a younger girl next to us whose family was smart – they actually brought money and planned their escape. They prepared how they would go about the whole thing bringing clothes, money, and everything they would need. There was a little market in Galang so if people had money, they could buy food or pretty much any of the things they wanted. But we didn't have any money.

The day started out pretty typically. It was about 110 degrees Fahrenheit, and I was miserably hot, sitting in our barracks, looking out the open door like a window, watching the little girl from the smart family as she dreamily ate a green apple and drank a cool 7UP her parents had bought.

I still see her so clearly, sitting there, cool and happy in her baby blue, thin cotton pajamas. She was a sweet girl, just eating that apple, oblivious of me drooling while I was watching her. *God, if I could just have a sip of that 7UP and a bite of that apple, I would be in heaven!*

I was miserable. We didn't have much of anything. So I cried to my sister, "I really want that apple and a 7UP! Do you think we might be able to get something?"

My sister didn't even look at me, "Are you crazy? You know we don't have any money at all."

I cried and cried to my sister because I was so miserable. I was the baby of the family, and I used to have plenty of my own money when I was running the restaurant. I used to be able to do all kinds of things when I was back in my old life in Vietnam, but now I'm sitting here drooling over a green apple and a 7UP.

My sister was 12 years older than me so she was 25 at that time. One day I saw her hanging out with a young man in the refugee camp and I got upset. I said, "You are married. Why are you seeing somebody else? Your husband is back home." They were writing letters. I was really, really mad at her and I wouldn't let up.

Finally she blurted out, "My husband left me! He had an affair! He is with somebody else now. He was supposed to escape with me, but he changed his mind at the very last minute. That's why I went to Mom and Dad that night and they told me to take you instead." As I already said, I didn't know I was not in the original plan. It was total luck that I got to escape from Vietnam. It was total luck that I was able to be in the picture.

My sister had a thin gold wedding band. It was the only thing she possessed besides her clothes. The next day she came back to our room with a green apple for me, an apple for her, and a 7UP for us to split. She had sold her wedding band to buy me a green apple, "It's bad memories for me anyway," she said after a sugary sip of 7UP, "Getting rid of it will help me release that emotion."

At that moment I was in heaven. After months of the same bland fish, flour, eggs, and beans, the taste of that 7UP was so powerful! I can still taste it. At a time in my life when I didn't have anything, that's all I wanted. I could have died the next moment and I would've been totally content; that's how happy I was with that green apple and 7UP. I later realized that the simple desire had planted in me the passion to one day become successful, make a lot of money, and buy everything my heart desired.

In camp, every day blended into the next. They were all the same filled with the exact same daily activity — waiting. But every weekend, we would go to the beach. That was my best memory of Galang: the beach! In my little mind, the trip to the sea seemed like an eternity. We would climb up mountains and walk down long roads covered with canopies of pine trees. Walking barefoot over all those pine needles hurt my little, soft feet like crazy. We'd have to wake up early and it took a long time to get there. To me, it seemed to be the longest walk ever, along endless dirt roads, and by the time we got there I was completely worn out.

I'd lie down on the sand, stretch out on our towel, and soak in the sun, listening to the sounds of lapping waves for a long while. We brought bread we made with flour and water, and put sugar on top to make it caramelized. This we savored as a little feast on the beach because that was our favorite place, our little slice of heaven.

It was an express trip to paradise every time we went to the beach. I'm still drawn to go to the beach every chance I get. The beach is where my dreams come alive. It is where my inner child can play and express herself without fears, judgment, or worries. Back at the barracks, everything was pretty depressing. But when I was at the beach, I came alive. I was able to feel that one day I could be me again. I got to dream about the day when I would be able to go to another country. Imagining what it was going to be like, and how much fun my life would be. It was my only source of joy in those days at Galang.

I couldn't have known it at the time, but that's where my BEACH Success System was born, from the magic of the sand and the water. I will tell you more about the BEACH Success System later. You see, when I'm near the ocean or water, I am totally energized; I can feel my being, I can see who I truly am, I can feel myself more than when I go anywhere else.

My special relationship with the beach began for me at 13 years of age on the beach in Galang. This was the only place where I didn't feel any pain, where I wasn't feeling miserable, where I wasn't just a number at a refugee camp. At the beach, I felt like I was in paradise.

After almost two years of waiting for paperwork, and trying to get a country to sponsor us, we finally got sponsored by the U.S. It was a miracle! How did this miracle happen? At that time, even though my brothers and relatives were in the United States, they didn't have the ability to sponsor us. The person responsible for getting us sponsored was my father, and he was able to do it by sheer luck.

During the war between South Vietnam and North Vietnam, my father had been a driver for an American army officer. Our family was blacklisted because he was seen as being related to the U.S. government. My oldest brother was also a pilot assisting the United States Military, so that didn't help either because the North was looking to punish the families of those who helped the Americans.

In 1975, when North Vietnam was about to take over, my oldest brother asked everyone in my family to escape from Vietnam with him on his U.S. government cargo plane, but we didn't go. My father and mother said, "It won't be that bad, we are all here. You go with your family. We have everything here- our house, our extended family, and our younger children." So they stayed and kept us all in Vietnam while my oldest brother and his family got out and went to America.

Of course, when the new government came into power, they put everyone through an identification process and looked into their history, what people did before they arrived, etc. So they learned that my father had been a driver for a U.S. Army officer. The result was our whole family getting put on a blacklist.

Little did we know that being put on the blacklist would be our ticket to getting out of the refugee camp. We had to prove to the consulate that our father had driven for the U.S. Army officer. We waited for two long years to obtain that proof, but once we did we were sponsored by the U.S. in only two days.

This is a clear example of how adversity can be used to your advantage!

People would chide my father about his decisions, "You should not have been involved with the U.S. government. You wouldn't have put your family on the blacklist," but nobody knows what the future will bring. This is exactly why I tell people that whatever adversity you are experiencing, accept anything and everything about it. If something is happening to you, at you, on you, whatever it is, accept it completely. Whatever consequence, whatever it is, deal with it, feel it, and be present with it. I am glad I accepted it all because I would not be here today if I had not.

It was amazing how fast everything seemed to move once we were officially sponsored! They sent us right away to Bataan, Philippines to learn English.

It was 1986 and everybody in that Bataan refugee camp was happy because they knew they were going to America. The teacher, Mr. Carlos, was a very nice, very loving Filipino man who spoke with a British accent.

I didn't speak any English at all, only Vietnamese. The first word they tried to teach me was "Hello." It was impossible for me to say. I tried and tried and tried, then finally I just said, "Hi" instead, because it was shorter. We were there for six months learning English, and by the end of it, I could say, "Hi" and "How are you?"

Then the day came, in April of 1987, when they put us on a huge 747 airplane in passage to the U.S. If anyone met me then, I said, "Hi. How are you?" That was the end of our conversation.

Chapter 3

Shameful Innocence

"Every single thing that has ever happened in your life is preparing you for a moment that is yet to come." –Unknown

---

In April of 1987, at 15 years of age, I first stepped foot on American soil. Part of me was happy to be in America, and part of me was scared. Now that we were going to be reunited with my family members, who had been living in America for years, I was worried that one of my relatives would once again try to do the terrible things to me that he had done when I was young.

At the age of 7 years old, a male relative molested me on numerous occasions for over a year's period of time. I was too young and innocent to comprehend what was happening or what he was doing.

One day when I was in the marketplace, I overheard people talking about a brother and sister, "He should never touch her private parts." I started hearing about family members who "slept together and now they have two babies," and "Oh, my God, that's incest. That's bad. Taboo!"

After overhearing those conversations among the adults, I started to feel ashamed about being touched and kept that secret to myself. Soon after the molestation started, he left for the U.S. very suddenly. In my child's mind, I made the correlation – what he did to me was socially unacceptable, so he had to be sent away. I was worried. What if people found out I was involved? Would they send me away from my parents too? In my innocence, I felt my secret was safer because he was no longer in Vietnam.

As I was about to land in Houston on my first visit to the U.S., my old fears started up again. This male relative and all the rest of my family were supposed to come and pick up my sister and me at the airport. For the first time since he left I was going to be facing this person again. What am I going to say? Nothing? Don't look at him? Don't talk about it because it's taboo? These naïve, isolated thoughts plagued me as a young teenage girl.

Back when I was in the refugee camp, I got my period for the first time and I remember thinking whatever he did — touching me like people had talked about in the marketplace — must've caused me to bleed now! I'm bleeding so much. It was so shameful to me that I didn't tell my sister I was bleeding. It was my period, but I had no idea what a period was, so I kept it secret. I didn't let my sister know that I was having my periods at all. After all, it was in the same area down there. I didn't know what it was down there. I just saw it was bleeding.

It was about this time when I started getting very spiritual. *God, can you please take pity on me and stop this bleeding?* I put a bunch of old clothes and rags and stuff down there, to stop it from bleeding, but it didn't stop, no matter how much I tried. I always avoided my sister those days. I went to somebody else's toilet and hid there. Then the third day, it was gone.

Thank you, God! I promise you I will be a good girl. I won't tell lies to my sister. I'll only lie about this bleeding to my sister, but nothing else!

Over the course of six months, it was like a confession to God every month. After the sixth month, I finally broke down and told my best friend at the camp, "Something happened to me when I was little, and now it seems like I'm bleeding every month because of it."

She said, "I know what to do. I'll help you. Your sister has this 'thing' she puts in her panties."

I didn't even know what panties were! My other friend said, "Oh, that's the thing that holds up that other thing! I have an old one — I was going to throw it away — you can use it."

I was 14 and had never learned what a pair of underwear or a bra was. So I said, "Great!" I was happy to get her old panties to hold up the cotton pad.

By this point we had been moved into Galang Two, which is the section of the camp for people who've been there more than a year with no country to sponsor them, no country who wanted them. It's like a village for the unwanted. (Galang Three was when you were dead. That's where they buried you.)

The good part was, in Galang Two, my sister and I had a little bit more room because we were staying longer. My sister had a chest she put things in, so my best friend, Thuy, said, "When your sister's not around, go into that hideout of hers. She has this thing that you can take and you can cut it up and tuck it up in there, and then when you are done and it's full of blood, you throw it away, and it disappears after three days."

It was magical! I was so happy, and it seemed like my problem was over and nobody was any wiser. That lasted for two months.

One day my sister and her girlfriends came around and said, "Utny!" That was my nickname, which means little baby. *Oh my God, did she find out I stole it?* This was the first time in my life that I stole anything. *Oh my God, I'm going to be in so much trouble because stealing is unacceptable. But I only stole it because I thought I was going to die!* That's when I learned that I will steal for life and death reasons.

My sister showed my one of her sanitary pads and asked if I knew what it was. I told her I didn't. She explained that she'd had six, and now had only four. She asked if I'd started bleeding. I told her, "No. No bleeding at all. Just last month."

I didn't want to tell her because of what I was thinking. Here I was, a little terrified girl, afraid I was dying, bleeding to death for months, and I wouldn't tell my sister because I believed that it was a result of shameful things that happened between me and my relative. Things I heard from people in the marketplace had created these false Beliefs in my mind, deep shame that scared me to death.

I have a friend who was sexually molested at 7 years old by a 16-year-old neighbor boy. He told me that, when it was happened, he did not comprehend that it was a bad thing. When he became a teenager and started to learn about sex, it was like he had to relive the painful experience again.

That is when he started to feel the shame. As a child, he believed that he must have been bad and was put through that as punishment. He never told a soul about his abuse until he was 43 years old, and married with kids. He held that inside for all those years because of the shame and guilt he felt. He finally shared it with a friend who had also been sexually molested because he was tired of holding on to the shame.

By opening up about it, he was able face the guilt and shame from something that he had nothing to feel guilty or shameful about. Be mindful this happens to so many people.

Odds are, you talk to someone every day who is holding something inside based on an outdated belief from a long time ago. They are living their life with a mask on that hides their pain, and they end up being a prisoner in their own fears and shame.

Beliefs are so powerful — which is why they are the very first step of the BEACH Success System. Beliefs control your thinking and they can control your whole life, but we will get to that shortly.

So, back to when I arrived in Houston, I was scared that I would see that relative again for the first time in years. It seemed like I was dying. I didn't want to see him because I knew now that what he'd done to me wasn't right. I was completely comfortable being around other man in the world back then, but I didn't feel comfortable around certain male relatives. I made up my mind that I would not sit alone talking to men in my family. Especially that one, because I didn't know what would happen, if he would do those things to me again.

I didn't see that relative after all because my oldest brother Phat, the one who had been a pilot for the U.S., came to the airport with his wife to pick us up and we stayed with them for the summer.

Their house was maybe 1,000 square feet; we lived there with them and their four children. They had a car and a little business that manufactured eye patches. The garage was their warehouse.

From the street the house looked like a shack, but the work done inside produced money to send kids to college and to Vietnam to support our family. To this day my brother would never sell that house. It's his "lucky money house."

Given all the money that he and his wife were sending to Vietnam to take care of our family, my brother had a big family and big responsibility on his shoulders. He was barely able to get by supporting his wife and four kids in those days, and he couldn't also support my sister and me. Shortly after we settled into a corner of their living room, my sister and I were driven to the welfare office in downtown Houston. An official there interviewed us in Vietnamese and gave us ID cards. Pretty soon we started getting welfare checks and food stamps.

I was shocked! I can't believe this country! They just give you money to buy food? I was so grateful.

I was amazed every time my sister and I would go shopping. I remember being so happy seeing all the packages of food lined up neatly on the shelves. We had money to buy anything we wanted! It was only a little more than a year earlier that my sister had to sell her wedding ring to get us a green apple and a 7UP. Now we could have anything!

I didn't know that people looked down at those on food stamps. One day, when my sister was paying with our food stamp coupons at the cash register, a lady was behind us in the checkout line, and I waved to her, my usual happy-go-lucky self.

All of a sudden, I could see it on her face that this woman felt we were beneath her, a lower class. I felt small and having the lady look at me like that made me feel even smaller for having to rely on handouts from the government.

I went home to my brother and asked, "Are welfare and food stamps bad?"

My brother put down the eye patch he was sewing and looked at me with tenderness, "People are not proud to be on welfare and food stamps, because it's only the poor people who get it."

I didn't understand that completely, but I internalized it to mean that people will respect you if you make a lot of money. In my head I started to believe I needed to make a lot of money so that I could have the respect I lacked.

When the summer ended and the start of the new school year approached, they began debating over what to do with my sister and me. My brother in Houston had four children, and my uncle, a religious leader, lived in student housing at seminary school, and his wife was pregnant. Neither one of them really had room for us, so my sister and I went to stay with my brother Matthew, his girlfriend Janet, and my other brother, Thanh, in Durant, Oklahoma. All five of us lived in a 400 square foot, one-bedroom apartment.

Matthew is a genius. He finished three majors in 3 1/2 years of college - mathematics, computer science, and another one, too. He was also teaching at the school. He is the brain of the family, and works for NASA now.

I had dropped out of 6th grade, so I missed grades 6, 7, and 8, and here I was in the U.S., barely speaking the language. Because of my age, they put me in the 9th grade. Matthew tried to tutor me; that was tough. My brother was so smart; he could not imagine why I was so stupid.

One evening we were working on math and the question he asked me was one I'll never forget, "What is negative 6 plus 5?"

I answered, "Eleven?"

He shot me the question again, annoyed. "What is negative 6 plus 5?"

I answered again, "Eleven!" *Why do you want to be so negative?* I'd never heard of a negative number. *Why would you want to add negatives? Why do you do that? I don't understand.* "6 plus 5 is 11."

Wham! He slapped me across my cheek so hard I actually saw stars! Then he screamed at me, "You are so stupid! You are the dumbest person I've ever known in our family!"

After that, I went out and truly tried to find out the answer to negative 6 plus 5. That energy of being upset fueled me to study hard. After he slapped me, it didn't take me long to figure out what negative 6 plus 5 really was. His girlfriend helped me the same night.

I studied my behind off because, when he slapped me and said I was the dumbest person in the family, I was mad and it fueled a desire to do really well in school.

I was translating day and night — English to Vietnamese and Vietnamese to English — because when you translate from English to Vietnamese it doesn't mean you understand what you're reading. I had been in a refugee camp for two years, so I didn't have the knowledge of math.

For years I was fueled up from Matthew's anger. I didn't realize it at the time, but I was harnessing the perceived negative energy to move myself closer to my goals of being smart and successful.

After just a few months of living with Matthew, he graduated from college and was moving to Houston as he was offered a job working for NASA. My sister now had a boyfriend and was living out of state, so only half of the "problem" remained: they had to figure out what to do with me. My oldest brother said, "I have four kids. I can't take her, so who wants her?" It was a horrible feeling; no one had room for me. I felt unwanted and unloved. Finally, my uncle, who was in seminary school in Fort Worth, Texas, said, "Send her to me, and I will take care of her."

My aunt was naturally quiet. When I first moved in, I tried to establish a relationship with her. One evening I saw her sitting alone on the steps behind the apartment. I walked out and tried to sit next to her. She quietly got up and walked away. I didn't know if she was finished sitting or didn't want to be with me. I couldn't blame her. Here she was, newly wed, and now newly burdened with my presence.

I was too young to have much insight, but as a child I translated every emotion into an internal understanding. It was the fuel that drove my desire to speak English well enough to have an intelligent conversation with somebody. That would be so cool! Just to have a conversation with an American where we can understand each other. That would be a dream come true!

That's why I tell people even if a dream is small at least it's a start. You need to go for it, to get started. This process of accepting of a small desire will set the course for the bigger dreams to be realized.

At first, my dream was just to be able to have a conversation. I was the new kid at a high school in Fort Worth. I couldn't speak the language very well, and therefore had very few friends.

After school I always wanted to get away, but had nowhere to go. I couldn't drive; I was only 15. I had my friend drop me off at the Water Gardens and I would wait there, all by myself, for my uncle to get off work and pick me up.

At the Water Gardens, I would sit and daydream that I was on my own beach. I would pretend that I was back at the ocean in Galang, dangling my feet in the water. I did that every day after school as I dreamt becoming very rich. I made the choice one day that I would secretly be successful and I wouldn't tell my uncle; he couldn't get mad at me if he didn't know.

One day I'm going to go for it, make a lot of money. I'm going to show my family that I can take care of myself. Everyone is going to want me around instead of not wanting me there. They will die for me to come and visit them, and they will miss me when I'm not with them.

All of this fueled my desire to be someone successful. That was my next level of dreaming after the desire to have a taste of an apple and a sip of a 7up in the refugee camp. I went through the war in my head because of how everyone around me made me feel; that was another defining moment. Trust me, in life, we will have many defining moments that will help build our character.

Chapter 4

BUDDHA AND JESUS

"Faith, hope, and love. But the greatest of these is love."

–1 Corinthians 1:13

"True love is born from understanding." –Buddha

There were three of us living in a tiny two-bedroom student apartment. I slept in the bedroom where my uncle studied. We didn't have much at all. Mostly what we had was Jesus. We talked about Christ all the time; my uncle talked about Christianity constantly.

He made every effort to convert me from a Buddhist upbringing to Christianity. There were constant conversations about how much Christ loves us, and how He died for us on a cross. Everything was about Jesus. Imagine how tough this was for me, having grown up with my mom, who was a Buddhist. She took me to the temple to pray every night and every day for the well-being of our family. I even prayed to Buddha to please help me escape from Vietnam and to let me safely get into the U.S. I promised Buddha I would do anything for him if he would get me to America alive. That was the deal I made with Buddha, and now here I was under constant barrage from my uncle to accept Christ and forget Buddha. Such conflict!

Inside, I loved Buddha. I just loved him! It wasn't like worship, just love. For a long time when I was little, I thought that, when I grew up, I was going to be a Buddhist nun. It was my dream because it gave me so much peace inside to be in an environment where people were not making comparisons or being judgmental. They were being very present, very Zen.

Here I was in America, going to church and studying the Bible. It was in Bible study that I first learned about the Sermon on the Mount and that Jesus was a teacher of love and compassion. Th is inspired me because it gave me hope that I was loved by Christ unconditionally.

I fell in love with Jesus and His teachings even more the day I learned about 1 Corinthians 13, which talks about my favorite subject- love. Christ was becoming my new best friend; I loved that the teachings of Christ were in alignment with my spiritual upbringing.

It was really the three of us all the time; Jesus, Buddha, and me. I always loved what Buddha lived and taught; he was all about love and compassion. Buddha was about the simplicity of life. Buddha talks about love and compassion, while Jesus talks about love, forgiveness, and salvation.

I met with people who were Christians and missionaries to other countries. Their good works helped me to love Christ very much the same way the Buddhist's good works did when I was young.

One day, all of sudden, I got word that my uncle, whom I was living with, who was a religious leader, went to Vietnam and ransacked my mother's altar. He threw away all the Buddhas on her altar. My mother was heartbroken. I understood that he was trying to help my mom see the love of Jesus and see that she does not need these Buddhas.

My mom told me, "Your uncle threw away all my Buddhas on my altar that I prayed to for his safety to escape to America." I was thinking, *my mom is 80-some years old. Why would anyone try to evangelize her this way? Why would he want to go back there and disrespect her and force her to conform to his new faith?*

That's when he forced me to think, *Christ, you know you are my friend, you are so loving. So why is my uncle so mean?* Reflecting back on 1 Corinthians 13, I didn't understand the reasoning for my uncle's actions. I understood his intention; he was coming from love. But I did not understand why he took such a drastic action toward an old woman.

What would Jesus do? Would Christ do what my uncle did to my mom?

As I reflect back now, I can see the BEACH Success System coming into play: the Beliefs. It keeps coming back to that again. Some people take their Beliefs to the extreme at all costs. In my world, my Beliefs that I live by are simple and bring more peace and love to me and to those around me. And if I can't bring them peace and love, at least I won't harm their wellbeing.

1 Corinthian 13:13 became my guiding light: Faith, hope, and love. But the greatest of these is love.

This is when I started questioning my religious life. There had to be something more to it than just being religious. I started focusing on being spiritual and going deeper. I began to ask deeper questions about myself and my relationships to my spiritual masters, Christ and Buddha.

I remember reading in the Bible where Solomon was praying for wisdom. Yes, that's it. That's all I want to know. I want to have wisdom more than anything in the world because, with wisdom, I will be able to understand why people do what they do. I felt pain when my uncle hurt my mom as a result of his spiritual Beliefs.

I feel hurt any time I see injustice or pain. I thought to myself, *why couldn't my uncle just go with the flow with my mother? You don't have to believe what she believes. Just go with her flow, let her live. She's 80 years old. Here you are, believing something new; you believe in Christ, and that you'll go to heaven. What makes you think that she is not going to heaven just because she never believed in Christ? What happened to the people before her? What is God's plan for the people before Jesus?*

We had a knock-down, drag-out debate about this; I had so many questions.

I will speak my truth. I will ask my questions. I will go to the limit with everything in my life; that's how I am where I am today. I am willing to go there, no matter the ending destination. I'm not scared. I will go to the most uncomfortable territory. I will share stories that most people wouldn't share.

I will share it all because I am so happy with everything that has happened to me. When I say everything, I mean everything; the good and the bad.

I started reflecting on all of the painful things that had happened in an attempt to understand why people chose to hurt me. I was beginning to unravel and understand why these things happened to me. The beautiful part about it was, the more I understood about myself, the more I had compassion and love for others.

For example, I now understand the psychology behind why my male relative molested me.

Growing up in a house with 10-plus people, I'm sure my mom and dad must have had sex sometime. My siblings and cousins must have seen them; they were just imitating what they saw. They were teenagers so they were curious about their own sexuality and their bodies.

I don't know what the real story is. His actions occurred while he was a teenager in effort to satisfy his own urges. I have so much love and compassion for him now. I am not saying that what he did was acceptable or OK. Just that I forgive him for the sake of my own well-being.

I understand this consciousness now because I'm watching nature play its part with our young son. One day, when baby Cash was two and a half years old, he ran into the room.

He was playing with himself, and asked, "mommy, mommy, what is this, mommy mommy, what is this?" pointing to his private part. I responded, "That is your friend, buddy, your friend is happy, that's all." Cash retorted, "Wow, mommy, my friend is happy all the time!" I told him, "I know sweetie, he is happy all the time because you are so happy." "I know!" he said.

I made sure to bring no shame to him and to let nature run its course. In my teenage years, shame was all I knew. Because my uncle was a religious leader, I felt safe with him. I told my uncle what happened to me- my whole childhood molestation story. He screamed, "Oh my God! Who did all this to you?"

I told him the name of the relative who molested me. He was so upset! His face turned bright red and his body shook. He started telling me I would never find a husband because I was no longer a virgin. Then he started sobbing and ran out of the house. To this day I am bewildered that my uncle seemed upset that I was no longer a virgin more so than concerned for my well-being or displaying any disdain towards a relative who molested me.

The next day I had a conversation with my uncle. If dealing with what happened was not bad enough I had to deal with his limiting Beliefs as a 16 year old immigrant girl in a strange land I did not fully understand. Although he was sorry about what happened, he was more concerned about the fact I was no longer a virgin and that no man would ever want someone like me. He said my children would suffer and it will manifest in my future life. I was just trying to process being a kid in a new place, dealing with doubts and insecurities that every person felt at my age. I did not know what to do as I contemplated the hard life my uncle laid out for me.

This is a classic case of how limiting Beliefs are transferred from your family, and/or your environment, to your sub consciousness. Many times you do not even know it is happening; I sincerely didn't know what he meant at the time. I remember how horrible life was for that couple in Vietnam who were brother and sister. They had two boys and there was so much shame and so much pain for them and their kids.

I dealt with this limiting belief for many years. In my mind, I had fears that I would molest my own children if I were to have any! That was one of the reasons I didn't want any kids, because of the Beliefs, fears, and environmental factors that had been embedded into my subconscious.

For the first few months after my son was born, I would not clean his private parts for fear that I would do something stupid. All because of these deeply-embedded limiting Beliefs.

Chapter 5

The Rape

"Character cannot be developed in ease and quiet. Only through experience of trial and suffering can the soul be strengthened, ambition aspired, and success achieved." – Helen Keller

---

At the time when I lived with my uncle, we were on a very tight budget. One day I said, "Hey uncle, can we go out after church and eat Pho?" (Pho is a popular Vietnamese soup.) He replied, "Yeah, we will. Sometime soon." On Saturdays the three of us went and got fried chicken as a family, and this was considered "eating out." I remember looking at the price. It was something like $8, and Pho soup was almost $6 a bowl. I didn't know what he was thinking, but I did the quick math in my head; *three of us getting Pho soup . . . that'd be $18. But with this meal it's under 10 bucks.*

I thought to myself, *One day I will be successful and make a lot of money. I will be able to buy you a bowl of soup, and me a bowl of soup, and my aunt a bowl of soup. I'll buy everybody a bowl of soup!* Situations like this often reminded me of the apple and the 7 Up as the incident was the foundation of my dream to be financially successful.

Luckily for me some members of the church invited us out to eat at a Chinese buffet. This was my first time out at a real restaurant. I was amazed at the expanse of food at the buffet! It was a mind-blowing experience for me to see so much food and that I could eat as much as I wanted.

My uncle was so excited and proud to be a religious leader, so revered, his congregation treated his whole family to the buffet lunch. Today that type of Chinese buffet is a cheap restaurant, but back then I was amazed and he was ecstatic.

On the way home my belly fat with Chinese food. I said to my uncle, "Why can't we eat at restaurants like that every day? Why can't the church pay you enough money for us to be able to eat at good places like that all the time?"

He always answered, "Let me tell you something. I want you to focus on Jesus Christ. You either worship Christ or you worship money. You cannot serve two masters." Every Sunday we had this kind of debate, until one day I asked him, "Why can't we have Christ and a bowl of soup, too? Why can't we have Christ and love him, do anything for him, be like him, and have a bowl of soup as well?"

Uncle said, "Of course you can have a bowl of soup, but I don't want you to get blinded by money."

"Without money, obviously we can't buy food, so why is money so bad?" I asked.

"Money is not bad, but it is bad." He contradicted himself all the time; that's how I grew up.

He loved to go out to eat, loved wearing name brand clothing of which he could not afford because he had little money. At the same time, he discouraged me from studying business.

I was about to graduate from high school and go to college so I asked him, "What should I study?"

I thought it would be cool to do some kind of business, because I remembered the feeling of freedom while running my parents' restaurant.

He said, "No business."

This really upset me to the point of tears. "So what do I do now?" It seemed like he was more worried about me now that he knew I wasn't a virgin.

He said, "I'll pray for you. If you get lucky, you will find a good Christian who will marry you one day. To help you find a suitable husband, you should study something in college that will make you useful to him. If you ever get lucky enough to get married, that would be the biggest blessing ever. To give you the best chance to find a man who will accept you, why don't you study to be a teacher?"

"Why a teacher?" I asked.

"You see, if you ever get lucky enough to marry, then your husband may have to move from one city to another. You can move with him, and as a teacher, you can get a job anywhere."

So, I applied to Belmont University and spent my first year studying to be a teacher. I had to do a lot of speaking and getting up in front of classes. I was still learning how to speak English and there was a lot of paperwork and writing.

I told my uncle I was struggling, so he said, "Study math, because with math you don't have to speak a lot of English." Negative 6 plus 5 still didn't mean very much to me by my first year in college.

My uncle encouraged me to be a mathematics teacher and I said, "Okay."

I thought I was going to die. I still hate math to this day! Somehow, I managed to do calculus by sheer willpower. One day I went to my counselor and said, "I can hardly speak English, and I hate math. Is there anything I can do that's a better fit for me than mathematics and computer science?"

My counselor said, "I've got it. Accounting and Information Systems Management have easier math requirements. It's not so hard."

The funny thing is, to this day I still struggle to attach a file to an email. I can barely record conference calls! So that's how much courage it took for me to go through with Information Technology and Accounting as a major. After five years, I graduated cum laude using the same sheer willpower that got me through calculus.

My uncle continued to tell me I would be lucky if I got a husband. I began observing and learning about marriage, because he said nobody was going to marry me and that freaked me out.

I started paying attention to married couples around me; many of them were religious leaders and their wives. There was a religious leader who shared a story with me about how he married his wife because she was a virgin and he was so proud of it.

The wife confessed to me one day that while they were on their honeymoon, he slapped her. I was confused, perplexed. If she was a virgin, and he loves her so much, why would he hit her on their honeymoon? That was a signal for me.

I didn't know if it was true that you had to be a virgin, but because of what my uncle said, I began feeling worse about myself and my chances. I felt like no man would ever want me because of everything that had happened to me. Nobody would want me.

My first year in college, I began dating. He was my youth leader and very possessive. I liked him simply because he paid attention to me. *Oh my goodness! He pays attention to me, so he must love me. Maybe I am worth something?* I dated him even though I didn't love him because he had the most beautiful handwriting ever, and he paid attention to me. I found something in that.

He was my height . . . short for Vietnamese. It felt good that someone liked me. To my amazement, other people started liking me too. I was shocked when other boys liked me; I didn't know what the heck they saw. Obviously something was wrong with them if they liked me.

I got into an argument with the possessive boy. He punched me so hard that the whole left side of my face was swollen like a football. My college roommate and best friend, Elaine, still recalls the incident 22 years later.

I went back to the dorm and Elaine immediately wanted to press charges. My head and whole face was bruised and I decided I was going to leave him. I wasn't clear in my thinking because I was so new at this entire dating thing. While I was dealing with this situation, I was crying and thinking maybe it was my fault. I began thinking, *Maybe I should be with him because he is my boyfriend, or I should have done what he said. It was my own fault he hit me, I shouldn't argue with him.* All this justification as to why he beat me up.

A few days later he called, very apologetic, and said, "I'm so sorry for what I did. Can we please, please talk?"

It was about midnight and he took me for a ride in his car. "I'm sorry I hit you. I'm sorry, but I love you so much it makes me crazy." You know, all the roses and chocolate stuff.

He drove us to Radnor Lake in Nashville, Tenn., and parked the car at the edge of a cliff overlooking the water. Then he took my seat-belt and wrapped it around me and around the back of the seat twice, and plugged it in so I was trapped. He pulled out a knife.

He then started to threaten me with a strong and firm tone, "You want to leave me? Fine! We are going to die tonight" By this time it was about 1 or 2 o'clock in the morning and it was very dark. With the car parked at the edge of the cliff, he pressed on the gas pedal and on the brake at the same time. If he were to let go of the brakes, we would die. If I would have tried to run away, he would have used his knife.

I was terrified, trembling, and crippled by fear. I was afraid for my life. I was watching his foot on the brake and the gas at the same time, revving the engine.

I was thinking to myself, *is this how I'm going to die? I'm going to die now? Wow, beating me up was not enough? Now I'm going to die too?* He said matter-of-factly, "This is it. Tonight is the night. I want to die with you. If I can't have you, no one else will."

That moment seemed like an eternity. Finally, my survival instinct kicked in, and my inner Hero came to my rescue. This is another moment that my inner Hero gave me permission to lie to save my life! It was not in my nature to lie. My inner Hero gave me clear, life-saving instructions, *Kim, just act like you like him! Use your feminine Energy to soothe him. It's not smart to fight him right now. He has a knife, and you're safer playing along with him. This is the one shot you have to save your life.*

But my fearful self kept screaming inside; *What am I going to do?*

Tell him that you love him, act like you do, and play the part, my Hero soothed.

I mustered every ounce of my courage, turned around and said, "But you know I love you!" I played out my part like an actress. *If I am believable, I will live; if I can't act believable, I'm dead.*

I made believe and told him "I love you. I just didn't like the fact that you hit me. You've got to be real with me about what you want. Just don't ever hit me again, please! I love you and want to be with you forever!"

Of course, he turned around and unbuckled me and we started making out. Imagine that moment. I was already disgusted with him, but to save my life, I did the whole thing. From making out to having sex. One day you're making love, the next day, it's rape. Everything is perspective and intention.

When it was all said and done, he drove me back to my dorm. I have never felt so messed up. I was crying. I had never felt so dirty. I almost died and now this horrible guy was all over and inside of me. I cried the whole night.

I was afraid for my life, so the next time he called I told him I didn't want to see him any more. That's when he became totally obsessed with me and began stalking me to the point where he faked his death and wrote a note he tucked in his shirt pocket saying that I killed him. If anybody found him dead, I was the one who was responsible.

One Sunday afternoon after church, a police car pulled up outside the sanctuary and two police officers got out and found me among the crowd. They had come to talk to me because he was in the hospital. He had tried to kill himself. They found the note in his pocket and wanted to know if I had done this to him. After that, every other boyfriend was a disaster. I had one bad relationship after another.

I tell women that any horror they may have gone through, I've pretty much been through it, too. So I know and I believe them. Even though I sometimes think I wouldn't believe my own story if it hadn't happened to me.

As a former victim, take it from me: we don't want justice, we just want to be heard and believed. Sometimes that hurts more than the pain itself. Many victims think their family and friends don't believe their stories of victimization so they keep their secrets inside. That makes it very hard to heal. I was blessed to have a few family members and friends who believed my stories. But that was only because they too had been victims.

Many victims kill themselves, self-medicate, and/or self-mutilate to release the mental pain as a result of the shameful feeling from not being heard or believed. The best thing anyone can do for someone who comes to them with a story of being victimized is to tell them that you believe them. Look them in the eyes and say, "I believe you."

Chapter 6

Tony... How Much do You Make?

"The important thing is not to stop questioning; curiosity has its own reason for existing." – Albert Einstein

---

Because of my excellent grades in college, I got a job offer as an underwriter for Cigna Healthcare before I even graduated. That wasn't the only job offer I got. The FBI tried to recruit me because I spoke Vietnamese. The Secret Service wanted to train me to become an agent. I was so naive at the time.

I went for my interview with the Secret Service not knowing if I would ever be willing or able to do what they were about to ask of me. The agent interviewing me asked, "Would you be willing to die for the president of the United States?"

"No, sir."

"Will you carry a gun?"

"No, sir, I won't."

He adjusted his tie in frustration and said, perplexed, "Then why are you here?"

"Because my professor told me to apply. He said that because I had a high GPA and I'm bilingual that I could get a good job."

"Not here."

The agent looked at me like I was a complete idiot! That was probably the shortest and dumbest job interview of my life.

So I took the job Cigna Healthcare offered me as an underwriter, crunching numbers. I learned enough skills to do the job, but I hated it. I spent two miserable years as an underwriter. After my first year on the job, I felt trapped in a cage with no escape in sight.

I had dreams of making six figures, but I didn't know how it was going to happen at Cigna. When I started there, I was making $28,000 a year. After my first year's performance raise, I was making $28,600. Wow, that was really disappointing! *How long is it going to take for me to make six figures working here?*

In the summer of 1997, I went to have a talk with my boss. I was armed with the resolve to break free from this cage. I said, "Tony, can I have a few minutes?"

Tony was a middle-aged good old boy with gray hair. He always wore a white shirt with khaki pants and suspenders. He had a corner office with nice furniture. I thought for sure he made a few hundred thousand.

I sat down in one of the two chairs facing his desk and said, "Can I ask you a question?" I asked.

"Yeah, what?" Tony replied.

"How much money do you make?" Tony looked at me like I was crazy.

I asked again.

"Why do you want to know? You are not supposed to know how much your boss makes. That's inappropriate. You don't ask those questions!"

"I'm sorry, but could you let me know. I have a reason" I said.

"What's the reason? Do you want my job?" he asked.

My eyes widened in surprise. If he only knew how much I hated my job, he would have fired me on the spot. "No! I just want to know because I have this dream of making six figures, and I want to know if I can do this with Cigna?"

He kicked back his chair and started laughing! I felt like an idiot. "Are you for real?" he asked.

"Tony, this is my dream! How long is it going to take?"

"You are out of your mind, girl. But now I see where you are coming from. I'm making $65,000," he said.

"$65,000? And you've been here how long, sir?"

"Twenty something years."

Now I was the one laughing, although I had to control my outburst in order not to offend good old Tony. "Tony, what do I have to do if I want to make $100,000?"

This question made him laugh at me even harder! Finally, he stopped laughing and said, "I have no idea."

"Tony, I want to make six figures, and you're my boss, so you need to show me how."

"Well, Kim, it's never going to happen in underwriting for Cigna."

"Then tell me in what department can I make $100,000?"

"You have to go to Atlanta and get into sales."

"Sales? What do I need to do to get into sales?"

"Are you kidding? You barely speak any English."

I said, "No, I'm not kidding, I really want to make $100,000."

"You have to do presentations, and you have to talk."

The presentations and public speaking was intimidating. "Is there anything else that I can do to make $100,000?" I asked.

Just then, a woman named Marsha poked her head into Tony's office. She was an outspoken and vivacious black woman. She said jokingly, "Oh, she wants to make $100,000..." and started laughing at me!

Then she said, "Girlfriend, you would do well in real estate. You're likable."

I am a freedom-seeker. I risked my life to search for freedom. Beyond that, I continually search for freedom when I sense either that I have none or I am losing freedom. While working as an underwriter, although I helped a lot of people, I felt trapped. To top it off, I was living paycheck to paycheck. I was single, but I made enough to pay rent and utilities, and send a tiny bit of money to Vietnam every month. By my second year at Cigna, I started to feel restless and in need of seeking a broader horizon, so I set out to explore other options.

Side note: When you start to feel that you have limited or no freedom — whether in business, personal, or spiritual pursuits — it's time to begin exploring other options. You always have options and choices in life.

I was grateful for having a job that paid my bills while living in America, but I wanted the freedom to have more. I was in acceptance of my current situation, and at the same time I knew I had to explore my choices; the choices that would give me the opportunity to reach the six figure income that I wanted.

All my life I have watched Inner Peace Outer Abundance being played out, over and over again. For example, with my parent's restaurant, we made a pretty decent amount of money. With the money we had, we always went to the temple and did charity work. That is how we found Inner Peace. Mom would go and give back from the abundance of our family. She helped people who were sick by picking and collecting herbs, which were used to create medicines. She always helped the poor people; my dad was the same way.

We had a ceramic jar of water available in front of our house for the thirsty pedestrians that couldn't afford to buy their own. This was common practice for folks in third world countries. My dad always taught me to give back and this jar has been a tradition of his for years.

Most of the time, my brothers or the elders would go to the well and fill up the jar. One day, when I was getting back from my morning trip to the local marketplace, my dad called me over to him, "Utny, today is your lucky day. I want you to fetch the water and pour it into the jar."

I complained that it was too heavy. I told him to get my elders to do this job because they were bigger and taller. He said, "Yes, I could do that, but I want you to do it. Do you know why? Because I want to build wealth for you in heaven. I want to build so much wealth for you in heaven that when you are ready to cash it in, you're going to be loved by all the gods."

So I said, "Ah, loved! Okay, I can do that." So I went and carried water from the well and poured it in the jar.

One day, some kids in the neighborhood threw a little turd in the jar and contaminated the water within. Guess who got to clean it? My dad only had to give me a look. He said, "Those people can build their wealth in heaven, or you can."

I said, "I'm going to build my wealth in heaven." That is how my dad helped me start to appreciate Inner Peace Outer Abundance. Do something to help others; both of my parents worked hard and made it a priority to serve others every single day. That has been one of those lessons I have carried with me all my life.

For the time I lived in the U.S. with my uncle, the Outer Abundance part of my life was absent. My uncle said, "The Bible says you cannot worship two Gods. You must only worship God, and not money." To him, money was a rival of Christ.

I had a fight with my uncle, a big fight, when I told him I wanted to become a real estate agent. To him, it was okay to be an underwriter and I should be happy to have a good job. But I wanted more. I wanted Outer Abundance, so I thought I should go try to find something else that would pay me six figures, such as real estate.

My uncle protested, "Business people are cutthroats. They do things unfairly." He gave me a list of what bad people would do for money. "They will lie, hide the truth, steal your client anytime, and all in worship of the so-called almighty dollar." I was confused, because I remembered my mom and dad as being business people, pure entrepreneurs, but they were always honest and never cheated people.

I thought maybe this was an American thing that my uncle was trying to protect me from. I had sought council in a friend who tried to encourage me by saying, "Everybody is selling something, including your uncle." This confirmed what I had been thinking all along! It was comforting to know that my uncle was "selling" Jesus to everyone every Sunday.

Chapter 7

The Grand Jury

"Courage is being scared to death… and saddling up anyway"

– John Wayne

While I was still working at Cigna Healthcare, I got involved with Dan, a guy whom I thought was a big improvement from the others, or so I thought. Dan was a bodybuilder and he taught me about health and wellness. He encouraged me to go to the gym with him and we worked out all the time…I mean all the time. He was from New Jersey and he used to curse like a sailor. One day he sent a package to me at my office. All I knew was what he had told me: "Can you pick up a package for me if it's sent to you at work?"

"Yeah, of course, I'm here all day. I'll pick it up and bring it home." We were living together at the time.

That afternoon, at about 1 or 2 o'clock, I went down to the mail room and looked around for the package he had described it to me. I saw a package that was open, so I looked inside and saw all the stuff he had described. I said to the mailman, Curtis, "That's mine" before closing it up and taking it back to my desk.

Within minutes, the whole office was buzzing about how security was looking for me. I called Dan, "What was that I just picked up? Security is coming for me."

Dan shouted over the phone "Oh, my God. Give them back the package. Tell them you don't know anything about the package."

I asked him, "What is it? What did you send here?"

He said "Why was it open?"

"Because there was no name on it. The person who sent it forgot to put my name on it!"

It was a shipment of illegal steroid drugs. Since Cigna knew it was an illegal drug, they naturally started thinking I was dealing drugs. They got the DEA involved, looked at my history, looked at my background, and even interviewed my college professors.

I had no record of anything, not even a traffic ticket. All of my professors loved me; I had graduated cum laude after all. The idea of me being a drug dealer didn't make sense. Then they found out my boyfriend had a record and they figured he must have been the one who sent the package in order for me to receive it. After questioning me, a representative in the HR department said, "If you want to keep your job, you need to give him up."

I called Dan on the phone and told him with no malice, "Hey, they want me to say that this is your package. I'll get to keep my job, and they said they will deal with you privately."

That's when he first revealed his secrets. He had a criminal record, and if anything else went onto his record he would be sent to jail for a long time. This would be his third strike. He had been caught dealing drugs twice before. He said, "If I go to jail this time, I will stay there forever."

I don't know what it was about me at that time — my innocence, my loving nature, whatever. I know that people who serve time in jail and have a record have a very difficult time getting a job and adjusting to society. Then I thought about my job, and my thought process went like this: *I never liked numbers or my job anyway. Should I risk holding onto something I don't like, and condemn somebody to jail? Who the heck knew when he would get out, and how old he was going to be when he got out?*

Maybe he would never get out at all? So I sacrificed my job for him because we were dating and I loved him. I'd find something else to do.

Dan coached me, "Your name is not on there, so you can say the package is not yours. The package is legally not yours."

I said, "You are right. It was never my package in the first place!"

I went to Cigna and said, "Sorry, the package is not mine."

They told me, "We know it's not yours." Here again, my hero jumped in and told me to tell my truth.

I replied "Then why are you accusing me of having drugs sent to the office? Why are we sitting here?"

This unfortunate chain of events was the trigger that helped me develop the confidence that would later become one of the biggest assets of my life. I had to fight those people for what I believed was true.

I lost my job immediately and, instead of going to work each day, was staying at home and dealing with the DEA. "It's not your package, so we know it's your boyfriend's package, because he's 300 pounds and his arms are 21.5 inches. We need you to help us put this guy in prison. Look at his record."

Literally, the DEA came and showed me his record. The DEA agent said, "Ma'am, I'm sorry, but you took possession of the package. If you don't turn him in, we will take you in front of a grand jury, and the grand jury will decide your fate." I was petrified when I heard that I had to go before the grand jury and testify. I clearly remember that day when I appeared in front of the grand jury. It felt like 1,000 eyes staring at me. It was an awful experience and a true test of my resolve to stand firm in the face of adversity.

I don't remember anything except that they said, "Ms. Kim Ha, do you know what 'perjury' is?"

"No." I had no idea.

"Perjury is lying to the court. Do you know what the sentence for perjury is? Jail. For many years."

My God, Jesus, and Buddha... this is where I really need you. Help me out. Help me, help Dan. I just want to help him. My court-appointed attorney coached me to tell the truth- that it was Dan's package.

But for some reason, my inner Hero was telling me that if he got sent to prison, it would do him much more harm than good and I would feel guilty forever. I felt that our prison system was dysfunctional and did not truly rehabilitate people. It made the majority of people worse than when they went in.

So I decided on my own to just stick with the fact that my name was not on the package, and that Dan really didn't force me to do anything, which was the truth. They asked, "Did he hold a gun to your head and tell you to do all these things?"

He didn't. I did it of my own free will. So I said, "No he didn't. He didn't do anything like that."

They kept asking me, over and over, if the package was mine: "Ms. Kim Ha, you looked for this package. Why did you look for the package if the package wasn't yours? Admit it was your package."

I wouldn't admit it. "It was not my package. My name was not on it." The mailman and everybody in the mail room testified against me, saying the package was actually mine because I saw it, I opened it, and I picked it up.

The only thing that saved me was the fact that, at the end of my questioning, I looked up at all the faces of the grand jury and said, "The package wasn't mine," I kept a straight face as I told them, "My name was nowhere on the package." That was the only thing that kept me from going to jail.

I stuck it out. The grand jury let me go, and now here's the real juicy part of this story: A couple of months later, I woke up and went outside to get into my car and I saw a beautiful pink greeting card with a little cassette tape inside the envelope tucked under the windshield wiper.

Dan must be trying to give me a little romantic surprise. So I opened up the envelope and it was a Valentine's Day card. It was summer, so I thought it was strange for him to be giving me a Valentine's card in the middle of summer. I put the tape in the cassette player of my car only to hear Dan's voice talking to a girl about how much he loved her. He was having an affair while he was dating me, while he was living with me. He was with another girl the whole time. There he was on tape telling her he loved her; that I meant nothing to him!

I listened to every word of that tape sitting right there in my car in front of our home. I couldn't believe what was on that tape! I began crying so hard. I became a total wreck. Before Dan, there was another guy I had been dating on and off in college who had also cheated on me. He was a doctor whom I loved so much. And he cheated on me! And now Dan cheated on me. I thought he was going to be different, but he turned out to be the fifth bad and abusive boyfriend in a row.

I was about to go jail for him! I just went through all this stuff to keep him out of jail, and now I hear him talking on tape about how much he loves this other girl.

"Kim is just a good girl."

I was just a good girl. That was all I was to him. The other girl framed questions on the tape so they would do maximum damage to me.

"Who do you love?" she asked.

Dan said, "I love you and I love Kim, too; she's a good girl. Let's not talk about Kim; just talk about us." She recorded that conversation because she wanted to hurt me, and she did. Listening to that tape made me so angry and heartbroken that I wanted to throw up.

After that, I became numb. I just went through this whole ordeal for him and he still cheated on me! Nobody loves me and nobody will ever truly love me. I looked in the mirror and I thought *maybe my uncle is right?*

After three days of crying and being totally heartbroken, I looked in the mirror and asked myself, *why do other women have a good man and I can't seem to have a good man?* Then I asked myself the key question that marked one of the most important turning points of my life:

Who do I have to become in order to have a good man in my life? How can I have a man that will love me, and won't cheat on me, won't kill me, won't hit me? Is it even possible to have a man that will love me, worship the ground I walk on, and adore me? It seemed impossible for me at the time.

I looked in the mirror and it seemed like no one loved me. There are only two people that I know love me - Jesus and Buddha. No one loves me, but at least I can love myself, can't I?

That's when my inner reasoning started, my insight kicked in. That was the beginning of my inner journey, when I decided to question my current situation.

Can I love myself?

I don't know, but let's try.

This is a relationship I'm going to keep. Just to see what it is like.

Right then and there, I decided I was going to love myself no matter what.

I was in my darkest moments, channel surfing, crying, and dealing with all of this while Dan was at work. I was sitting on the floor and I saw a personal development guru on TV at 2 in the morning promoting the idea of taking charge of your own life. "Are you ready to change your life? The past does not equal the future."

I ordered his personal growth tapes and started listening immediately because I didn't know what else to do. The guru said, "You have to be positive to attract a person who is positive."

He talked about creating a list of the things you want in your man or woman. I felt hopeful. Somehow, I got the courage to start a plan to get my life back. I began to see the light at the end of the tunnel.

I took a look at my current situation and the things I wanted to be different.

I wrote down: "This is what I want. I'm going to end this relationship. From this point forward, I'm not going to waste my time with any man. I am going to go on a journey of personal power, to gain personal power for me. I want to have my power."

It started out as just a dream, but this was my true journey. That was the defining moment when it all started. The next day, I wrote my list of what I was looking for in a man. I listened to those tapes religiously and this part hit me the most – when talking about "a list," obviously if he doesn't meet the criteria, then I have to end the relationship. I gathered my courage and was finally ready to confront Dan.

"Dan, I just want to say thank you for loving me, and I don't want to hold you back anymore. I want you to be with the girl you love the most."

"What are you talking about?" Dan was puzzled!

"I want you to be with the girl you love the most, because you obviously don't love me." I slapped the tape into his hand and told him, "This is it. I'm done."

I went into the bedroom and started taking all my suitcases to the front door. When he saw that I was really serious, that I was packed and I was actually moving out, he went into his office and came out with a gun in his hand.

"If you leave me, I'm going to shoot myself right here." He was standing in the front door, trying to block me from leaving. "I love you, I don't love anybody else. That tape was all just a lie," and on and on. "I'm sorry," he said „This is all a mistake. You know I love you. I only want to be with you. I don't want her. If I can't be with you then I'm going to blow my head off!"

He went on and on, frantically trying to explain what had happened and convince me that he loved me. But I knew that, even if this had all been just a big misunderstanding, something deep inside of me had already shifted, I was beginning to feel my self-worth increase, and realized that I deserved much more. Certainly much more than Dan could ever provide.

As Dan tried to stop me from leaving, I gathered all my courage. Feeling at peace, I told Dan, "You know what, Dan? You know I don't like blood.

You keep threatening that you're going to kill yourself. Just f*ing shoot yourself right here. But don't expect me to clean up your mess!" I pushed past him and out the door I went.

That was the first time in my life that I ever used the F- word, and that was the last boyfriend who ever did anything to hurt me. Dan used the F-word all the time, so I became numb to it. When I used it for the first time, I felt powerful. This was the first time I stood up for myself and it helped to create a powerful trigger word in an intense situation.

Most people don't have a very favorable impression when they think about their ex's. Not me. I love all of them, because all of them made me who I am today. Even the one who raped me and tried to kill me. He made me discover my Hero, and who knows? Without him, I may have never tapped into that part of myself. It is easy to let go of what you don't want when you appreciate the impact it has had on your life. Each of my ex's has played a vital role in my growth and have truly helped to shape me, and I am forever grateful for their contribution.

Chapter 8

The List

"It is necessary, and even vital, to set standards for your life and the individuals you allow in it." – *Anonymous*

I continued listening to my personal growth tapes daily. The guru talked about the past and how it does not equal the future. So I took a hard look at my past. Obviously, I spent a lot of time thinking about my uncle's proclamation that in order to be worthy of a man's love and commitment to marriage "You must be a virgin."

I started testing all my preconceptions about life and living, and that's when I started focusing on my inner work, and focusing on becoming more of me. I was not sure who Kim was, so I was on a mission to find out. *Who is Kim? What can she do? What does she love? What does she like?*

The guru said to make a list and write down what it is you want and what you have to do to make it happen. So I made a list of what I wanted and who I would need to become in order to accomplish the goals I had set out for my life. I even made a list of what I wanted in a man; at first, the list was very short. It got longer over time.

My grand vision was to be happy.

I had to start with small steps, *I want a man who:*

Won't hit me.

Won't cheat on me.

Won't lie to me.

Someone who will text me or call me back (because my ex Roger, who had cheated on me, never returned my calls or texts).

The man I described in my short list would be so good! That's how I taught myself a very important concept: start from wherever you are. For example, I recently coached a client named Algeria whose husband abused her for six years. I asked her to imagine a man who wouldn't hit her at all. If I would have told her to imagine she was with someone who is "a good man," or some other all-encompassing concept, it would be too big for her to grasp or even imagine.

I said to Algeria, "Imagine there is a man who won't hit you at all, and will tell you that you are a good-looking woman, and that he likes you."

She said, "That would feel so good."

I asked her, "What else would you like to see in your future man?"

She said, "He'll tell me I'm pretty."

After hearing that, I knew that she liked to hear words of confirmation, so I gave her some. I told her, "As a matter of fact, I'm going to tell you right now you are a pretty girl. You are very pretty and sweet. You have beautiful hair. You have beautiful features, beautiful eyes."

She was pregnant and about to give birth, so I added, "And you are one of the prettiest pregnant woman I've ever met!" Within a week, she wanted to leave her husband of six years because I was the first person who understood what she was thinking, and that gave her empowerment. Everyone in her family had been trying to get her to leave her abusive husband for years, but they didn't know how to talk to her.

Most people around us and in our family will tell us, "He is a bad man. Leave him. You deserve much more." That's not clear language and instruction. Before my coaching session with Algeria, she would have never understood the concept of deserving much more.

I spoke to her in her own language, keeping in mind the same kind of very limited thinking I experienced myself when I was in her situation. That's the only language she could understand, and at that moment, she needed to hear the same language that was going on in her own head. That way she could pull herself up a little bit and step up to leave him less than two weeks later.

What I did was walk Algeria through the BEACH Success System, which you'll learn more about later. I've noticed many times how powerful the BEACH Success System is, especially compared to traditional therapy. Many therapists struggle to get that kind of result for a client so quickly.

Why? Because therapists use psychology and terminology that most people don't understand. They can't understand a girl like Algeria. No one understood her because they hadn't been in her shoes. They didn't understand her psychology from a human perspective, from the perspective of a real person who went through the same kind of harsh experiences she was going through. She needed someone who could empathize with her.

So if you're reading this right now, and your man (or woman) is hitting you, just put on your list that you want someone who won't hit you. You cannot tell someone who is being battered that they should go and hide.

You may not be having a relationship issue. You may be having an employment situation. So on your list you might put down: *What would I like from your employer? Would they offer certain benefits? Would they provide a flexible employment conditions?*

Have a grand vision to move toward. Your inner child or loving child inside of you or your higher self (all the same to me) always knows what you want. Take small steps to get started; we have to start with simple, manageable steps that we can put into practice right away.

When I look back, my first list was so humble! Back then it seemed like a strange new world. When I started with that list, I still remember wondering *how can I ever find this amazing person?* Then I started looking around at my life and breaking it down into bite-size elements.

How do you find anybody to date you when you're at work all the time?

Someone told me about online dating services. At first, I thought online dating sites were for losers! I thought it was for people who couldn't find a date in real life, so they hid behind their computer and posted fake pictures.

When I learned more about it, I realized it was the perfect vehicle for me to experiment with dating. I had little time and wanted a place to share my intentions and my list.

I went to a dating site online and completed a profile. "I want somebody who is . . . " I listed out all the items I had written down and typed in "Someone who will return my call. Who won't cheat on me." The whole list.

I got a few dates, went out with a few guys, and found out that guys were into me. After a while, I began to gain a bit of confidence. *Somebody actually wants to go out with me!* I met guys who were professional, handsome, and educated.

After a while, I upgraded my list.

Confidence isn't built overnight, and we don't break out of our limited Beliefs overnight. Our confidence can't come back in just a week. I watched it build back up slowly, and I upgraded my list over and over again.

I learned that it is best to start with the very simplest thing, wherever you are, and then continue to upgrade and update your list. You have to make some choices. You can't start at the top of the world, because right now, your energy does not line up with a person who is on top of the world.

I told Algeria my whole story. I pointed out all the abusive guys I dated throughout my life and she started laughing. I said, "That's the best I thought I could do at that time — why else do you think I would live with any one of them? You think I was stupid? Yes, maybe I was at that time, for that moment."

I told her about a lot of my exes, and we laughed about it together. "I dated him, and here is why. But I upgraded and I upgraded until I got to a point where I upgraded to my ultimate list of 45 items. It was a 12-month process, and I upgraded multiple times."

Not every person I dated had everything on the list. One person had one thing, the next person had something else. This guy had this and that, but I wanted this other thing too. That was how I did it. Dan had some attributes I liked, but then I upgraded. I wanted Dan's height, and a guy who worked out, but I also wanted a guy who would have other qualities.

I went on lots of dates! From doctors, to lawyers, janitors, to factory workers, engineers, to entrepreneurs. And I started to notice a pattern. What I was most attracted to was their intelligence and their passion for their work and their life. It didn't matter to me what they did for work; what mattered most was their passion.

Around this time, I started to make more money which became an important qualification, too. At first, income didn't matter, but after a while, I wanted to date men who were financially successful. It wasn't even about the money. It was about their confidence, their intelligence, and their ability to create wealth; that was really sexy to me. Eventually, I would only date somebody who was earning equal to or higher than my income. The ultimate list had a qualification that I wouldn't date them unless they were making at least $120,000. I thought to myself, "Who the heck is going to be making $120,000 besides me?" That was when I started to feel special.

The ultimate list included the requirements that he had to be physically fit, emotionally mature, financially successful, and spiritually awakened. On the physical form, the man had to have perfect hair, perfect teeth, and be 6 feet or taller. He had to have real teeth. He had to be spiritual. There were 45 items! I made no exceptions on my list.

By this time, I had transformed myself from this weak, naive girl whom guys walked all over, to a highly sought-after bachelorette (long before the TV show first went on the air!)

I reached a point where I had spent an entire year working on myself, dating lots of different guys, going out and building both my self-worth and my net worth. I had built myself up with all kinds of self-development studies, such as Tony Robbins' materials. I read Brian Tracy, all the books by Zig

Ziglar, anything and everything that people would recommend to me. I especially loved Napoleon Hill's *Think and Grow Rich* and Dale Carnegie's *How to Win Friends and Influence People.*

After one year of online dating, I got to a point where I stopped dating just to date. I realized that, instead of going out with ten boyfriends in the next five years, I wanted to go through ten boyfriends in one month. I wanted to collapse time, so I could find out what I really wanted.

So I updated my profile online: "I believe in honesty, and I want to be able to date different people. No exclusivity during this time." Before that, I dated one guy for a few months and went through a breakup; it cost too much time.

I set a clear intention to purify myself with God by taking a year off of sexual activity. I just wanted to go out, have fun, find out if there is chemistry and how many common interests we had in short amount of time. That whole year was a sexual sabbatical for me, and it was the most rewarding year ever.

I went through a whole year dating five to ten different men at a time. This was pretty cool. I was able to speed up the process and collapse time, so I could deliberately find my true love, the man who had everything I wanted. Th en I picked my five to seven favorite guys and set out to see which one was closest to what I really wanted.

I was able to keep it simple without too much drama because I didn't have sex with any of them, just dating and really getting to know each other well. I learned from my previous relationships that sex complicated things, and I wanted to dedicate an entire year to God to cleanse myself and focus on the other attributes I was expecting in my ideal partner.

The guys I would date according to the ultimate list would have to be 6 feet tall or taller. Previously, if a guy was a good man, I would date them regardless of their height, but I got to a point where they had to meet a physical requirement. That's what I wanted.

Then men started to want exclusivity with me; "Kim, I just want me and you." I heard that many times from lots of different guys.

"I can't right now," I'd reply. "I promised myself to go through this process for one year without settling for anyone. I like you a lot. You are one of my favorite guys. I've been honest with you this whole time, but I'm not going to settle for what is making me happy right now. I have to go through with my whole plan."

Then the dating list dwindled down to five favorite guys. I started telling my dates very specifically what I liked and what I wanted. "I like men who wear khaki pants and baby blue shirts. And I love yellow roses." All the things I like.

A funny thing happened: all of them were dressing the same when we went out on dates! One evening, a guy named Jarrett happened to be flying into town and decided to surprise me. He should have known never to try to surprise me, especially knowing I was seeing other people. He had called to check in with me that day, but I forgot. He said "What are you doing tonight?" I told him, "I don't know."

I didn't remember, but I already had a date with Duke that night. So of course Duke and I were in my house getting ready to go out when I heard the doorbell. I opened the door and Jarret walked in with khaki pants, a baby blue shirt, and yellow roses. He saw Duke, who was also wearing a baby blue shirt, khaki pants, and had brought me a bouquet of yellow roses.

They both knew I was dating other guys, so it should not have been a surprise to either one. The only surprise was that they both ended up at my house on the same night. Jarrett was from New Orleans and went to LSU; he was a radiologist. And here was Duke, an engineer. So I introduced Duke to Jarrett, Jarrett to Duke.

Jarrett said, "I checked with her today and she didn't remember what she was going to do tonight, and she said nothing."

Duke turned to me, gave me a look and said, "You forgot our date?"

"Yes. I'm sorry."

Jarrett said, "Kim, what do you want to do now?"

I told Duke to decide what we should do. He decided we should all go to dinner together. It was one of the most uncomfortable, awkward moments in my life. I told Jarrett to sit up front in Duke's Audi convertible. I sat in the back seat freaking out, feeling very nervous, and giggling! Shoot, oh shoot, what am I going to do?

Duke took us to my favorite Th ai restaurant downtown, and we all started drinking alcohol. It turned out to be one of the most funny and comical events I have ever experienced. It was like an episode of a sitcom on TV. We were chit- chatting, then they talked about their careers, and then they started talking about me, as if I wasn't even there: "Yeah, Kim is a great girl."

"Yeah, that's why I like her a lot."

"Me too."

Oh my God! They are talking about me, right in front of me, about how much they each care a lot about me. This was the most endearing and ego-building experience of all time!

When it was all said and done, Duke drove us all back to my house. Jarrett was going to be staying in my guest bedroom.

Duke said, "Why does he get to stay here? Why can't he stay at a hotel?"

"I guess he could," I said.

"Why don't you ask him?"

This whole ordeal was so funny. That's why I say I became the ultimate bachelorette. I was upfront with my vision and I removed the sex, which was the thing that was amazing, but that could also be confusing to some people. I was finally able to have it all; love, respect, and adoration from all my favorite men.

For the first time in my life I was finally creating my own Inner Peace Outer Abundance. I was intentional about my love and my money, and this was starting to change my life forever.

Chapter 9

Rookie of the Year in Real Estate

"Sweat equity is the most valuable equity there is." – Mark Cuban

---

Let me back track to how I achieved success and made six figures in real estate after I got terminated from Cigna Healthcare. Making that kind of money was one of my heart's biggest desires and goals. You see, I wanted to prove to myself, and everybody else who thought an immigrant girl from Vietnam did not deserve to think that big, that I was capable of anything so long as I continued to be passionate about my goals. I didn't know anything about real estate, but I took the opportunity and learned the skills day in and out.

Once again, I found myself at a fork in the road. I had a decision to make. Do I listen to everyone else's small vision for my life or do I listen to the voice of my inner child? Guess what? I'm humbled and blessed that my Hero is listening to my inner child's voice. My uncle did not approve because of his limited Beliefs about money and business people. He feared that money and business people would lead me astray and cause me to do unethical things.

I finally declared to my uncle the following: "Uncle, this is the kind of real estate agent I will be. I will be truthful. I will not steal people's clients. I will always disclose what I know. If I don't know, I will research, then I will tell them what I find. I will always protect them. I will be their agent for life."

My uncle said, "Well, that's all nice, but you are not going to make it. You'll see. Most agents don't sell any real estate in their first six months."

Due to the standards I set for myself, plus the intense effort in building my real estate business, I earned the Rookie of the Year award after my first year. Because I had an inner desire to treat my customer right, I went above and beyond the call of duty. I worked day and night to find them the perfect home. I never pressured them to buy a house. It was a great part of my success. I told them we would take as long as they needed, and once they found the house they liked, they would know it, and I would help them make the purchase.

People said, "Oh my God! Where did this real estate angel come from?" Sometimes we would look at 100 houses, which didn't bother me at all. I earned my reputation from how I treated people, and consequently, got more clients than anyone else. That was how I became Rookie of the Year. Again, it was not because I was smarter than other agents, I was just working harder than others.

I developed a nickname among my customers. They called me "The Lucky Agent." To this day, when many of my past clients buy a house, even though I am no longer directly dealing with real estate, they will still put my name on the sale, and I will still get the commission because they believe I bring so much abundance into the house. That is their belief. The last time this happened was in 2014 on a $1 million home! The buyers said, "You are the Good Luck Agent, so I have to buy the house through you. Because of the house I bought through you in the past, I have made so much money!" The word on the street is that if you buy a house through Kim, you will be blessed with abundance. That's the reputation I have earned in the Vietnamese community in Nashville for the past 15 years.

When I say I was working hard in real estate, I was sometimes showing houses as late as 11 p.m. or midnight. Some of my clients would get off work at 6, 7 or 8 o'clock at night and those were the only times they were available for me to show them the houses.

Many of my clients only spoke Vietnamese and I translated their mortgage applications as part of my unique service. I became proficient with taking loan applications in Vietnamese. Because I wanted the loan process to be faster so we could close the sale smoothly, I literally took a complete application. I gathered all necessary paperwork from W-2, pay-stubs, to bank statements and I put them all in order and turned in to the loan officer a totally complete file that was ready for process. In other words, my file was ready for the underwriter to review immediately.

One day, I got recruited by Ed Hoover, an owner of Titan Mortgage at the time. He asked me, "Do you want to be a loan officer?"

"I don't know how to be a loan officer."

I replied "You're already doing it, Kim. I saw your file, you've always turned in a complete file," he attested.

"Really?" with an embarrassed look on my face. I had no idea what a loan officer really does.

I was pleasantly shocked that they were willing to pay me for what I was already doing! As a result, I was able to add on another six-figure income from the mortgage businesses to my current, successful real estate business. My colleagues started to become jealous of all of the hard-earned money I was making. In 2001, my managing real estate broker came to my office and explained that I needed to pick and choose. She said, "You can only do real estate or mortgages. You cannot help your clients by doing both. You are not serving them."

"What do you mean, 'Not serving them?' When they don't speak the language, I have to do it all anyway. So why can't I get paid for that?"

"We won't let you do it."

One of my real estate colleagues, Jack Hitson, who was also an agent in the same ERA Real Estate office I worked in, advised me, "Call this guy over at RE/MAX. His name is Robb Campbell. He's a very progressive broker. Someone told me he lets his agents do loans and real estate at the same time. Call him and check it out."

First thing the next morning, I picked up the phone, "Could I speak to Robb Campbell, please."

"This is Robb Campbell." I skipped the pleasantries and went straight to the point- "Do you let your agents do mortgages and real estate at the same time, sir?"

"Yes."

"Okay, I'm coming right over."

I went straight to his office where he showed me the compensation plan. I immediately signed on to work for RE/MAX. I didn't look at or read anything. I just told him to give me the best plan he had. I showed him my volume, and what I'd been doing.

I asked, "What's the best plan you can give me?"

He said, "According to your numbers, you should be on this compensation plan."

I asked, "How much money would I be making compared to how much money I'm making right now? And, again, give me the best compensation plan."

He told me, and I believed him. "Wow, that's a lot more money I can make over here. Done. Thank you."

I shook his hand, and five minutes later I was out of there. The next day, I started at RE/MAX, and that was it. I loved the freedom I had at REMAX. The agents were professional and friendly. I continued to focus on helping my sellers and buyers, and doing a fantastic job with their loans. I quickly became one of Robb's top agents at RE/MAX.

Chapter 10

Never Say Never

"You don't know what you don't know"

– The 7 simple yet powerful words from an Anonymous Author

RE/MAX had its company Christmas party in December that year. The great part about being single was that I had a ton of freedom. The bad part was that, since I didn't commit to anyone, no one was really committed to me. All the guys I was dating at the time had gone out of town for the holiday to be with their families and nobody could go with me to the company Christmas party. So I asked my girlfriend Marlene to go with me. We were on the phone, just closing our last deal of the year. I said, "Marlene, RE/MAX has a company Christmas party tomorrow 7:00 p.m. at a Marriott in Franklin, and none of my guys are in town. I don't want to go alone. I barely know these people at RE/MAX. Would you go with me, please, pretty please?"

She said, "Yeah. That sounds fun. See you tomorrow." We went together and enjoyed mingling all evening. At the end of the night, she went home. I was about to walk out the door when I saw a group of single agents for RE/MAX, including Mr. Robb Campbell, milling about.

I went over and joined the group, and Robb was polite saying, "How do you like the company? How do you like the agents here? Kim, I am very proud of you and of the good job you're doing!" He proceeded to give me a little pep talk, then he continued, "A group of us are going to go out tonight. Do you want to go with us?"

Many of them were staying at the Marriott that night, so they went up to their rooms to change out of their dresses so they could go out. Robb and I sat at the lobby bar waiting for them to come back down so all of us could go together. As we were chit-chatting about business, all of a sudden, a woman came in with a big guy trailing a few steps behind her. She went ballistic, screaming at Robb, because he was talking with me as I sat there next to him. I was absolutely dumbfounded.

I didn't know what was happening. I had no idea who she was. I never met her before. It turned out she was his wife! So I immediately told Robb, "I hope Mrs. Campbell didn't think I was your date or girlfriend. Did she?"

"Oh, no!" Robb replied.

"Do you want me to go tell her I'm not? Who is that man?" I asked.

"That's her brother," he answered.

I asked, "You want me to go tell them who I am? I mean, I can go tell them."

The last thing I wanted was to be between them and create misunderstanding. It was not good to mess with the boss's wife. He said, "No, no, no....ah...um....we're getting a divorce anyway. You are actually the first person in the company to know, so please don't tell anyone yet." Because of what happened that night, we kind of shared a secret now, and we became a little closer as friends.

That night, and occasionally after that, we'd go out at night and have fun with a whole group as friends. We did singles stuff and took dance lessons, and became even closer friends.

A few weeks later, someone in our RE/MAX office suggested to me, "Hey, Kim, you should hook up with Robb." I thought that was completely disrespectful. In my culture, there were two main reasons why any woman would date a divorced man. Number one, the woman is getting older. In our country, that would be about 25-35 years old. Number two, she would not be as attractive, so the only choice she had would be a divorced man. Dating a divorced man was never on my list, particularly one with two kids.

I was very offended and upset. I walked into Robb's office one day and said, "Robb, let me tell you something. You and I are good friends, so let me be honest with you. I could NEVER date somebody like you. And let me tell you why. You are divorced and have two kids. And I heard your ex-wife is horrible. So I'm just letting you know, nothing will ever happen between you and me." He seemed surprised and didn't seem to understand my intrusion and proclamation.

Once Christmas was over, all seven of the men I was dating came back, so I was back to my normal rotation of men. Robb met a few of them. He was dating somebody also, so I started to give Robb advice on dating. I even gave him advice about what to do during his divorce.

"Here's what you're going to do," I said. "You're going to go out and have fun. Date a minimum of 10 women at a time. Don't commit to anybody. Tell them you're not ready to commit just yet. Just have fun exploring your options because you need to let this baggage go. Seriously, when you've been married for so long, and you date somebody, you don't want to just go ahead and commit right away. It won't work. Trust me. I'm pretty experienced with dating different people." I encouraged him to date a lot. Sometimes Robb and I even went on a double date together.

One time, Robb was taking a date to New York, and I went over and helped him pack. I picked out outfits for him. I said, "Wear this. She'll love that. Wear this to dinner, and after the show, take her here." I helped him get prepared for that date in New York. That was how intense and close our friendship had become. I told him how to treat a woman. I said, "The way to treat a woman is to first be a gentleman. Just because you're paying for dinner or shopping doesn't mean you should expect her to have sex with you. Be nice, and when the moment is right, if she wants more, she will let you know. The woman will let you know. Don't push for it." He agreed.

All the people working at RE/MAX could see what good friends we were, and they would ask if we were dating. We would always say, "No, no, we're just good friends. That's it."

One summer day, an agent invited Robb to a political dinner party she was having. Robb looked around and said, "Man, I don't want to take a date to a political dinner party. Since you're my best friend, can you go with me so I don't have to take a date? Just as a friend, so we can hang out?"

The host knew we were good friends. We got dressed up and went to the political party. Looking back, I'm not sure if he planned the whole night, but after it was over, he said, "Do you want to go to Nick and Rudy's Piano Bar? We can practice our dancing moves. You know, the ones we learned together." I thought it would be fun.

We walked in to Nick and Rudy's and Frank Sinatra's "Strangers in the Night" was playing, which was one of my favorite love songs. It was such a romantic place, with great ambiance, and the song fit the mood perfectly. As Robb and I danced, he kept giving me this sweet, kind, and endearing look. And I started feeling some strange feelings.

I was thinking, "Golly, where is this feeling coming from? He's divorced and you are still having these weird feelings." And as we danced I kept thinking, "Good grief! What is this weird feeling inside... this is weird. Very weird."

There was this odd and uncomfortable silence in the car as Robb was taking me home from Nick and Rudy's. We heard on the radio a commercial announcing that Phantom of the Opera was coming to town. I excitedly blurted out loud "Oh my goodness! I love Phantom of the Opera." Robb quickly replied, "Let's go!!!"

A few weeks later, we got dressed up again went to "Phantom of the Opera," and after the show, Robb asked me to go back to Nick and Rudy's again. This time the feelings got just a bit stronger between both of us. I thought to myself, *this is truly weird. You know if you ever date him, you're going to break up with him in six to eight weeks. That's your pattern; short-term relationships. You can't commit; you have not committed to anyone in a long time. That's not good. He's your friend. You can't break up with a friend if you date him. Don't even go there. He is a very good friend of yours now. Don't do it. No, no, no. Don't even go there! Besides, he's divorced. His ex-wife's horrible. And those two ungrateful kids you don't even like... Stop this feeling now!*

I was filled with conflict, so at the end of the night as Robb was taking me home from Nick and Rudy's, instead of inviting him to come inside my house to hang out like I normally would, I said a quick "goodnight." I got out of the car quickly. I was blown away by these emotions and feeling really weird about it. Why was I falling for a divorced man when I told myself I never would?

As a gentleman, Robb got out and walked me to my door. He gave me that endearing look again. I was feeling so awkward that I did not look up. Then I said "goodnight" again. I went inside the house, locked the door, and went straight to my bedroom. The next day, I didn't come in the office, and for months, I avoided seeing Robb at the office. If I saw him at the office, I tried to keep the conversation brief.

Thanksgiving rolled around and I kind of missed him a little bit. I thought to myself, *I never miss anybody! Good grief. I hope you don't fall in love with him. Good heavens - his ex-wife and two bratty kids! Please don't fall in love with him. That would be the last straw. I would be doomed!*

I remembered, *oh man, it's already Thanksgiving and I never even thanked him for the 'Phantom of the Opera.' I didn't even say thank you or good night. I didn't say anything. I guess I should call him and say, 'Hey, how are you?'* I was just making up excuses, one after the other.

The best way to tell the story is through our own words:

Robb: She called me on Thanksgiving while I was at my Mom's house. We had a great conversation and both of us caught up with what was happening in each other's lives. Things had been kind of awkward up to that point, and it was good to be talking again.

Kim: We kept our conversation very casual...

Robb: A few weeks later, we had the RE/MAX company Christmas party again. One year later. She came on her own and I came on my own. I was now officially divorced, so at the Christmas party we started dancing again, and there were those feelings again. I was having them, she was having them, but we didn't tell each another.

Kim: Neither one told the other.

Robb: So here we are at the company Christmas party, having all these feelings which are getting stronger and stronger, and about a week later I went to my mom's house for Christmas. I was supposed to stay a week. Arriving on Christmas day, I was supposed to have Christmas dinner, and stay a week with my family, but I got down there on Christmas day, and Kim and I were really missing each other, I was missing her, she was missing me…

Kim: ...I missed him a lot!

Robb: ...And after I had brunch with my mom and family, I decided to give her a call. We started talking and I told her, "I'm really missing you," and she said, "I'm missing you too." It got to the point that finally I said, "I'm just going to come on back." So I drove down there that morning, had brunch, and told my mom I had to go back, got back in the car and drove back. We haven't been apart since.

Kim: From that moment on, we knew.

Robb: I got in at midnight that night, and we got together and started talking, and …

Kim: ... we knew... we had held back for so long ...

Robb: By the first of February, we knew we were going to get married. It started snowballing from there.

Kim: All these guys I dated for so long... I would take every one of them to visit my brother. My brother would say, "Oh, I like him," and "Oh, I like him too!"... He loved every guy I ever brought home.

When I took Robb back to visit my brother for the first time, he told Robb, "Let me tell you something Robb, I give you 6 weeks with her. She usually dumps a guy in 6 weeks. So, good luck, brother."

A few months later, we started talking about getting married. Before Robb asked me to marry him, I warned him, "Robb, let me put everything on the table before we go any further. If you marry me, you need to know... I don't cook... I don't clean... I'm not going to take care of your kids. Are we cool with that? I have worked very hard to build my business and my wealth. I have helpers that do everything for me, like cleaning. I live a certain lifestyle and I'm not going to subject myself to cooking and cleaning and having to take care of your kids either, okay?"

His kids were so ungrateful at the time. They would ask things like, "What are you getting me for Christmas!?!? I hope it's not anything under $500!!!" They were around 12 years old. I am big on gratitude.

From that point on, we took on the challenge of helping both of Robb's children develop gratefulness and other values to the point where, at the age of 16, his son went to work to buy his own car. That was a transformation. Now I'm like a mom to them.

But, let's rewind back to the summer when we were supposed to get married.

Robb: In the Vietnamese culture, you have to ask the oldest male of the family for permission to marry. So we flew down to see her oldest brother in Houston to talk to him about getting married.

Kim: We knew that my brother in Houston did not want me to marry anyone but an Asian man! He had said that to me on many occasions, "If you marry anybody but an Asian, don't invite me to your wedding... don't even call me... no permission granted." So here we are flying down ...

Robb: I was freaking out. The first person we talked to was her brother's daughter, who's about Kim's age. Turned out she was dating a surgeon out of California — and luckily he was Caucasian. The daughter had broken the ice with Kim's brother! We got a chance to talk to him and asked his permission for Kim's marriage. He turned out to be the nicest guy, sitting there with no shirt on and a pair of run-down shoes. We had a great conversation, great food, drank beer, and finally he said, "All I ask is that you love Kim... I love you guys and wish you the greatest marriage."

Kim: When it was time to pick out a date for our wedding, since neither of us are good with numbers or remembering dates, I said, "We have to pick a date that's easy for us to remember, such as 12/12, or 10/4... or something practical." We looked at a calendar and looked at Oct. 4 of that year. It happened to be on a Saturday.

Robb: Oct. 4 (10-4) was on a Saturday... So we agreed, "Hey... a perfect day... we can't forget that date for rest of our lives, right? We decided to get married, and we got it planned. At the time, I had been living with my brother Jay since I'd gotten divorced. But now that we were all set to get married, I moved in with Kim. So we're living in Kim's house together, and my ex-wife says, "You guys are living in...

Kim: Sin!

Robb: My ex said, "You're not married. The kids cannot come to visit you."

She was all riled up. Sinners!

Kim: What constitutes sin? What constitutes not-sinning — when we get married?

Robb: We're all set to get married on Oct. 4.

Kim: We have the date set up already, but she insisted we couldn't have the kids visit us.

Robb: My ex was just being controlling. That's the way she was all the time when we were married.

Kim: I asked Robb, "Where can we get a marriage certificate so we can send it to her?"

Robb: Honey, we have to actually get married. So the next weekend we went down to Panama City ...

Kim: We took two friends with us, fun clothes, we got a minister on the beach, and got married.

Robb: On May 16.

Kim: The date we already told everybody was Oct. 4.

Robb: We didn't tell anybody about May 16.

Kim: We got the marriage certificate and faxed it to his ex-wife so she could send the kids for the summer and we could spend time with them. Then we continued with our plans to get married on October 4, like nothing was ever changed. In my mind, the real wedding was Oct. 4.

Robb: We had a "real wedding," and then our "show wedding."

Kim: Which one was the real wedding? Both of them are real to me.

Robb: The one in October was for us, in front of everybody. Her brother, Ngoc Ha, was the preacher who married us. He didn't even know about our first wedding.

The funny thing was that my husband Robb would never have made the cut because he was partially out of alignment with my 45-item list! One of my most basic values is that I would never date a man who is divorced or had a girlfriend he broke up with after dating her for 10 years. I believed that somehow the love between those people would be there forever... I mean, what if the guy wanted to go back to that girl at some point? I would get hurt again. So I refused to go there.

As you can see, the list was very helpful, but ultimately, there is a master plan for our lives and our love. Some of the guys whom I had been dating were upset when I got engaged, but I had to follow my heart's desires, and they all led me to Robb!

Chapter 11

The Shift

"If you are looking for the next big thing and you're looking where everyone else is, you're looking in the wrong place." – Mark Cuban

---

Robb and I started focusing on building RE/MAX, and we also opened a mortgage company and built it from scratch. In our area, we dominated the market. Since we both experienced a lot of success individually, when we came together we became a powerhouse. We poured all the money I saved before our marriage back into building these businesses. We grew to 15 RE/MAX offices total and had 400 agents. We also started a mortgage company, an insurance agency, a title company, a graphics company, an appointment setting service, and all these different businesses.

The businesses just took off and exploded. We pooled all our profits together and invested them back into the company. In 2007, we were the #1 Multi-office RE/MAX Broker Owners of the year for RE/MAX International, worldwide. We generated more than $1 billion in sales that year.

There we were in 2007, on top of our game, and everyone from the outside was looking in at us and wanting what we had. They said, "I want your houses, your money, cars, employees." Some people even told Robb they wanted his wife! But the stress level we were under was killing us. We had to make $329,000 a month to break even. Robb's blood pressure was going up and up and up and I saw this.

What started us on personal development (a side journey) was the death of one of our friends who was in the mortgage business. He was my age and had a wife and two kids, and one day he just up and died and left his wife and kids with nothing. This freaked me out. We knew we had to find a way to reduce the stress.

We were honored to be #1 in the world. We were being flown to Kona, Hawaii, and Robb was going to be one of the speakers. RE/MAX was asking us to help other brokers build their companies. Only the top brokers in the world were asked to attend.

We were on the beach in Kona, hanging around with all these men and women who were in the Chairman's Club of RE/MAX — which meant you had to be the top of the top, the cream of the crop. You had to have 100 agents or more, and Robb and I were being honored. We were literally sitting on the beach enjoying our success with all these top people, but then we got a phone call from my director of operations. I answered my cell phone, and heard, "Hey, Kim . . ." I could hear the trouble in his voice.

I immediately asked, "Who died?"

"Do you want the good news or the bad news?"

"You're on the phone, just give me both."

He said, "Okay, the bad news is that we just had a buyback."

Mortgage brokers who contract with a bank to lend the money to write mortgages are liable in the event that the mortgage goes bad. When a mortgage goes bad, the bank notifies the broker that they have to buy the mortgage back.

I was the CEO of our mortgage company so I said, "Okay, how much is the buyback loan?"

"$180,000. That's the bad news. The good news is, we don't have to pay it this week. We can write a check next week to pay out to the warehouse lender."

I got off the phone and tried to find Robb to tell him the bad news. He was pacing back and forth on the beach, sipping on his coconut drink, talking on his cell phone, dealing with a lawsuit. Somebody was suing us because they just bought a house with a two-car garage, and their SUV didn't fit. We got sued for that. As a matter of fact, that lawsuit turned out to be very nasty. It seemed to go on forever!

I looked around at all these brokers who were 20 to 30 years older than us, they didn't look happy or joyful, and I said to Robb, "These people are all miserable. What is our life going to look like when we get to be their age?"

Figuratively speaking, sometimes in life we're on a beach, but we have to ask ourselves is it really the beach we want to be on?

That day at the beach in Hawaii, Robb and I realized for the first time that we didn't feel happy with the life we were living. We didn't quite know what it was, but that strange feeling led me to listen to the inner child inside once again that was telling me something needed to change. An innocent voice of a young child has no judgment. I got that inspiration from watching little kids think and behave and, eventually, I got more confirmation from watching our own children.

We gave full attention to "something needs to be changed." Most people just push through these warnings and don't listen the soft voices from the inner child calling out the discontent in their own heads. They don't pay attention to the pain they are experiencing. There are fears that are worth facing.

For example, for every client I coach, I assess their fears and I tell them, "You shouldn't conquer all your fears. If the fear is worth conquering, do it. If it's not worth conquering, why bother?"

In other words, conquer only the fears that are aligned with your dreams, goals, and passions. As for me, I don't have a need to conquer my fear of heights by climbing Mt. Everest, but I did need to conquer my fear of public speaking.

I also coach my clients to be willing to question their current situation, whether it is personal or in business, question to see whether or not it is bringing them peace and abundance. If the answer is no, then explore your options, and follow your heart.

With RE/MAX, we could have gone on and built our business even bigger, but it got to the point where we weren't happy in the business anymore. It was tons of stress, and we didn't want that kind of stress in our lives.

There is such a thing as stress that's worth our time: when we're doing something we love and it's pushing us out of our comfort zone. But when we no longer find joy in our business or whatever project we are working on, then we are experiencing a negative form of stress, and this can be dangerous to our health. Stress can kill us!

It's up to you to know which is which for you and your life. Because we felt that something was not right with our lives, I told Robb, "Honey, none of these things matter to me. Being #1 in with RE/MAX, being the CEO of our mortgage company; none of that matters. All I want is for us to really figure out what it is that we really want to do for the rest of our lives."

The next day, we dropped everything, and sat on the sandy beach with a whole different mindset. We had no agenda. We just laid there and didn't pick up any of the phone calls coming in. We didn't care at that point. We just didn't know what we wanted at all. We were willing to let go of anything we didn't want emotionally. We looked at RE/MAX, and said, "We're making great money, but this is not the kind of life we want for the next 20, 30, or 40 years."

So there we were at the top of the game, looking for an exit strategy. As fate would have it, we were sharing our frustration with our colleagues and friends, Rock and Lisa, who were also on the trip. It turned out they were trainers for one of the biggest names in the personal growth industry, and suggested we attend the next seminar.

We attended several business seminars and became part of a platinum mastermind program. As part of that program, we got to go to Fiji for two weeks.

It was at the retreat in Fiji that we met a man named Srinivas who was the master, teaching thousands and thousands of people. He had been a monk for 14 years. He taught us about how our mind isn't our mind.

When he spoke, I listened and felt that he was speaking right to my heart. We fell in love with him and his teachings! Because of his teachings, I started observing my thoughts and facing all of the thoughts that I was once afraid to acknowledge.

While I was going through the process, I was really struggling with one particularly disturbing thought. There was a person in our class that I felt hatred toward, for no reason! As a Christian, I was taught to not hate anyone, so I was in agony.

I had to talk to Srinivas about it. For the first 20 minutes, I couldn't bring myself to tell him about this negative thought that I couldn't accept. He asked me "Kim, what thought is bothering you so much? You can tell me anything." I told him that I hated a person in our class, and that I felt horrible about it! He said nonchalantly, "It's okay. Is that it?"

I shouted back, "What do you mean, 'Is that it?' Hating is a sin, like a crime to me! I'm a Christian, I'm not supposed to hate anyone. I'm supposed to love my neighbor." Srinivas replied that it was just a thought, and to accept it and let it pass. It's okay to have the thoughts you are having.

It sounded too simple, and I didn't quite know what he meant, but it sounded right. The next day, I paid attention to my thoughts and I let all those thoughts pass me. Before, I'd usually try to stop a thought and admonish myself when I had such a thought. This time, I didn't judge ANY and ALL my thoughts for one day. To my own amazement, I felt so free. That was the first time in my life I felt so free and at peace.

I felt a profound relief in my body and soul, and a permanent shift in my perception. It was an awakening that changed me forever! The veil was lifted and it was like a breath of fresh air! I was now able to acknowledge and accept all of myself; all of my loving, not loving, and all so-called disturbing thoughts.

It was in that moment that I solidified the foundation for my Inner Peace. I had let go of judging my thoughts and had developed deeper compassion for many others. The next day, I started sharing my experience with everyone in our class in Fiji, and started teaching and guiding them through the process. Everyone came to me and asked me many questions about their passing thoughts. I smiled to them and told them, "It's ok." Like Srinivas told me, "It's ok!"

I'm a constant work in progress, but I am so grateful to have God's favor. I embraced Srinivas' message, and I am more at peace now than I ever have been in my life.

Chapter 12

The Traveling Monk

"The heart of human excellence often begins to beat when you discover a pursuit that absorbs you, frees you, challenges you, or gives you a sense of meaning, joy or passion." – Terry Orlick

---

After sharing so many deep, personal challenges, Srinivas and I bonded and became the best of friends.

One night after dinner, I asked him, "What is your passion? What else do you like to do?"

He said, "I like helping people. I like that I'm helping you."

I pushed him to get personal. "What's your passion besides teaching us about the workings of the mind?"

"I'd like to go around the world and take pictures. I love to see new places, every corner of the world, and I'd love to capture these experiences on film." As he was sharing this with me, his eyes lit up and his whole body shook with the passion of his love of photography.

"So when are you going to do that?"

"I don't know. Sometime in the future." he responded.

Then his energy sunk.

"Why not do it now? Life is about now, bro."

He was shocked and couldn't quite answer me. He hesitantly said "....uh...uh...I don't have the financial resources or time to do that right now."

At the time, we were at a spiritual retreat where we each had to pay about $10,000 to be there. As a business person, I had to ask Srinivas, "So, may I ask, where did the money go? The money we paid you guys to guide us. Do you get a portion of it?"

He quickly changed the subject and said, "Money is not important; we are here to serve and to give."

"So where does all the money go?" I asked as I started thinking about where all the money went. "There are 100 of us in this place right now, and you are doing most of the work, and you can't get to travel and take pictures and fulfill your dream?"

Srinivas said he didn't know and that it was not that important to know where all of the money went. I asked him, "Srinivas, what do you know about currency? Or money?" I kept inquiring about it. "Srinivas, don't you want to get paid for all of your hard work here so you can see the world?"

He said, "Money is not important and what I do is not business. It's spiritual."

I thought to myself, "with all the millions coming in from the work of all the monks, where does this money go?" It didn't make business nor spiritual sense to me. Srinivas told me again that money was not important to him, and that's not why he was there. He was there to be of service.

I finally concluded that Srinivas obviously didn't know about currency. I thought I could attempt to educate him about money and currency. "Okay, how did you get to this retreat? You had to fly a long way to get here. Do you realize that it cost money? Who's paying for your flight?"

He said, "I don't know, but we don't get paid."

I dug deeper, "How did you become a monk? What did they teach you about money when you first started in the order? I really want to know."

Srinivas replied, "Well, they taught us that money is the root of all evil. And that we should dedicate our life to our faith. We shouldn't get married. Oh, and sex is bad. Sex is a sin."

I asked him if it made any sense that the founder of the organization of the monks was married and had a son, and the son who is in charge of the order is also married and has a baby girl. "Did it ever occur to you that what they teach you and what they do are two different things?"

He hadn't looked at it like that before. The founders were collecting a lot of money from all the trainings with the free labor of the monks. If they paid those who delivered the teachings, Srinivas and I wouldn't have been having this conversation right now.

"Srinivas, you have brains, and you have spirituality, but they take advantage of you and all the monks because you have no knowledge of how business or money works. But you know what? I'm going to teach you to manifest Outer Abundance. We are going to find something you will love doing and can get paid for, then we can blend that business and spirituality together."

"Everyone should be compensated for their work. You have your own life to live and that should be honored. How are you going to plan to live your life without knowing money or currency? No worries Srinivas, one day we are going to do something big together. One day, we are going to mix business with spirituality, raising consciousness, and creating abundance. How does that sound?"

"Ugh, no thank you, Kim. I will be a monk forever," was his only response!

"Listen Srinivas, everything is energy, including money, and if we use it right, we are going to serve the world. We are not going to manipulate people and enjoy wealth while others suffer. I want everyone around me to make money. Nobody should sell themselves short so that I can live my life. With that belief, imagine what kind of world we could have?"

He smiled at me and said, "No Kim, I'll be a monk forever, my friend."

We laughed together at how silly the idea was because we had never seen a true blend of spirituality and business before!

After we left Fiji, we continued on our path of personal development. Srinivas continued to guide thousands of people in Fiji. During another one of these personal development seminars, we met a gentleman who introduced us to the travel industry.

He was sharing the idea of a wholesale travel concept. He was part of a company that was revolutionizing the travel industry by making travel more affordable for everyone. They were offering vacation packages at four- and five-star resorts for two- and three-star prices, and the quality and experience was amazing! That got my attention.

He told us their business was a word of mouth model and that we could build it as a side business or as a big business. We got to choose whether we wanted to make a few hundred dollars or earn as much as six or seven figures. Little did he know that I always loved to travel, so this sounded incredible to me!

As I studied this new, fun, and travel business venture, I saw the opportunity to help my friend Srinivas. He loves to travel and takes pictures around the world. Who else out there is looking to have more fun in their lives, create fulfilling experiences, and become financially free at the same time? We didn't realize it at the time, but we just found the business model that could launch our mission of Inner Peace Outer Abundance!

Chapter 13

The Bride's Nightmare

"In the midst of movement and chaos, keep stillness inside of you."

– Deepak Chopra

Looking back, I realized that my connection to Inner Peace Outer Abundance started when I was a child in Vietnam. I was earning my own money at 9 years old, which made me feel abundant. At the same time, I was constantly helping others who were less fortunate, often homeless, or mentally challenged. Serving as a child allowed me to embrace Inner Peace starting at a very young age; I have been doing so ever since.

Then I got to America. My uncle was sending me a conflicting message; money (a form of abundance) was evil and it was impossible to be in alignment with Christ and business simultaneously.

He would quote Matthew 6:24, "No one can serve two masters; for either he will hate the one and love the other, or he will be devoted to one and despise the other. You cannot serve God and wealth."

When I first began working and making money as an adult, this view of money expressed by my uncle was always a source of conflict in my mind. I wanted to be in business making a lot of money, and I wanted a powerful relationship with God. I didn't feel like I was "serving" money, but that money was "serving" me to follow God's path.

I was in constant turmoil, so Inner Peace was out of the question for me at the time. As I got older, the conflict continued to keep me from reaching my goal of Inner Peace. Even when we became wildly successful, it just didn't feel right; something was missing. Keeping God and money separated caused me to feel unfathomably terrible.

The straw that broke the camel's back was actually my wedding day! The church I was a ttending at the time was extremely conservative and had very strict Beliefs about what was acceptable.

"We are Baptist, so we do this and we never do that."

I loved flowers so much that Robb and I spent about $10,000 for our wedding flowers. Th e day before the wedding, a deacon told us, "We thought about what you are planning, and I'm sorry, but you can't have that many flowers. Your wedding day is about you, your husband, and Jesus. The union is far more important than the flowers. So we can't allow you to have that many flowers."

I almost fainted because the vision I'd always had for my dream wedding was a sanctuary filled with flowers. That was my dream! But because of the church, and their Beliefs, I couldn't have the one thing I truly desired to be in my dream wedding. We had no choice but to relocate the flowers to the reception area and have the wedding in accordance to their rules rather than our dreams.

After all was said and done, we were married and walking down the aisle as man and wife, I looked at Robb and told him with teary eyes, "When I die, can you make sure my funeral has more flowers than our wedding?"

I couldn't understand why an abundance of flowers would be seen by the church leaders as "unfocused" on God. My heart ached at the idea of this once loving and supportive church community being stuck in a box called "how we honor God". It seemed as though they were never going to step outside and embrace the concepts of worship and honor that were sitting just beyond the walls of the church building.

I was actually starting to question both the teachings of the church, and even Christ! Questioning Christ? I started praying and asking Christ: Is this you acting? Or is it the people? Can it be both? Could it? What is this?

Why can't I have You and flowers? You created flowers, didn't you? Why tease me? Why can't I use flowers to celebrate my marriage?

After a few months of contemplating my spirituality, and God, I stopped going to the church; I wanted to find peace and stillness without the influence of others. I wanted to get to know God myself.

God, I hope you don't get mad at me for leaving the church, but you are everywhere. You do mean everywhere, right? We are best friends now. You and I are on this journey together. I am grateful that now I will get to spend more time with you.

After I left, I did miss the Vietnamese church community and the fellowship. They were like my extended family. Because my relationship with God was so much stronger and deeper, I found that I didn't need to be in any particular place to feel and experience God. I'm not trying to discourage you from going to church; I do go to church here and there. I'm simply not dependent on the church to bring me Inner Peace or bring me closer to Christ. On my journey, I started really asking questions when I saw injustice or lack of authenticity.

My life's biggest struggle has been to find a way to have both Inner Peace and Outer Abundance simultaneously. Along my journey, I started to notice that others were struggling with one, or the other, or both! One thing I've witnessed in life is that there are a lot of spiritual people who are suffering financially. For example, they want to be helpful and adopt foster children, yet they don't even have enough money to take care of themselves.

On the flip side, I've noticed many others who have money, but are really stressed out. Look at wealthy people, stars, and athletes; they make tons of money, yet many of them are numb with depression and turn to drugs or alcoholism. The problem is, they lack Inner Peace. I started noticing a pattern and started asking, "How do you marry those two together? How can you have Inner Peace and Outer Abundance at the same time?"

I witnessed so many people, like Srinivas, who had great Inner Peace but no way to achieve Outer Abundance. I began feeling as though I was called to help everyone embrace both. For years after Srinivas had left the order, we funded his travel so he could visit family while still running his spiritual retreats to help others. If we did not help Srinivas, he would have had to beg for money in order to continue helping others with their spirituality.

One day I said, "Srinivas, we're willing to pay for all your trips. But being a man, how does that make you feel?"

Without hesitation, he replied, "I feel ridiculous!"

"Exactly! So why did you set up your life this way, being a monk, and relying on everyone to buy your stuff for you? You don't have the understanding that currency is energy, and energy is currency. Srinivas, everything costs money, and it's okay for you to earn money through your spiritual teachings."

This is how the Inner Peace Outer Abundance movement was conceived. I know "Inner Peace Outer Abundance" is grammatically incorrect, but I want you to know, Inner Peace Outer Abundance is like a marriage: two coming together as one.

Srinivas was the first monk we brought into our travel business. We helped him get started and taught him our business success system. We took him one step at a time from working through his limiting Beliefs about money, to being able to travel the world whenever he desired. He is currently traveling the world, enjoying his free time, and making an impact along the way. I'm so happy that Srinivas decided to partner with us! Working together on our Inner Peace Outer Abundance movement made it possible for him to travel the world and take pictures wherever and whenever he wants.

He just got back from a huge photography safari recently. He got to take all the time and pictures he wanted; to have fun and not worry. He has more money now than he's ever had before! Most importantly, he was able to take his mom to her favorite destination for vacation.

The Inner Peace Outer Abundance that I want for myself, and really for everyone, is to be our authentic selves while achieving our heart's true desires.

Chapter 14

Go to the Beach

"It is only in adventure that some people succeed in knowing themselves-in finding themselves." – Andre Gide

---

Many people ask us, "How did you do it? What's the secret to your success? How did you take two businesses, from very different industries, real estate industry and travel industry, all the way to the top? So many others have tried and failed, but you have figured it out twice!"

So I started thinking, how were we so successful while others were struggling in either industry? Of course there are many different factors, but as I reflected, I realized that one of the biggest contributions to my success was the adventure I endured by escaping my country, being rescued and dropped off in a couple refugee camps in Indonesia and the Philippines, and going to the beach to rid myself of the anxiety caused by the daily camp routine. The beach is where I started to dream.

I also realized that I had been following a series of guided principles to overcome challenges and become successful. The lessons I learned along the way would eventually develop into the BEACH Success System. I would go on to teach my system to thousands around the world, helping them to achieve their own Inner Peace Outer Abundance.

The BEACH Success System that you've been reading about is truly a divine inspiration! It's the Holy Grail of Inner Peace Outer Abundance. It was born on the beach in Galang, Indonesia, when I was at the refugee camp. It was at that beach that I had my first taste of freedom.

Today, I realize Inner Peace Outer Abundance is our birthright. We are born with nothing but love and joy in our hearts, but it is the scarce mentality of the subconscious which strips us of our Inner Peace Outer Abundance as we grow past childhood.

As I look back, I realize that every major decision in my life has been made at the BEACH, or during an adventure! For instance, Robb and I got married (the first marriage) on the beach, which is where I created the "concept" of Inner Peace Outer Abundance: on the beach in Hawaii. I also worked with Srinivas on my profound inner shifts while at the beach in Fiji. My body and soul feel at home there - on the beach.

For me, it was the perfect combination of the word that fit me best, and the principles in which I traveled through repeatedly on my journey to success. I have taken thousands of people through these steps and found that this system not only works for me, but has also been the key to guide many toward their own Inner Peace Outer Abundance.

There are two parts to the BEACH Success System: The first is to literally go to the beach, or get near a body of water such as the lake or pond! It's crazy how most people spend their whole life working and never physically touch the ocean. Anytime I meet someone who wants me to coach them or wants to be part of my movement, I immediately advise them to go the beach, especially if they have never gone before.

Often they protest, "I can always go later."

I say, "Just go, then come back and talk to me."

If the ocean doesn't resonate, then I suggest mountains, lakes, or burning a fire. The water or fire provides a calming e ffect which is necessary in order to get deep into your heart and open your eyes to the limitless goals which you truly desire. Some people I work with try to take a shortcut, but it is the most important step in the process. Clearing your head is a profound first step because it removes the clutter and opinions of others, allowing a clear path for you to take on the journey to discovering your desires. A simple dream, once voiced from the heart, can break any fear!

They say, "You want me to take time out of my busy life, take time off from work, drop everything and just go to the beach?"

The beautiful part is, when they come back they are always different. "Oh, my God! Why didn't I ever go to the beach before?"

It's always been that way. You're not only going to the beach, you're going to get back in touch with your inner child. Don't bring your cell phone. The beach is where you can experience the Inner Peace, because the serenity allows you to tap into your inner essence.

The beach is reminiscent of a simple time when we were children and would just walk up and down the shore. We can walk along the water's edge and start dreaming again. Stop thinking and start dreaming. The beach can be very soothing. When we are at the beach, we can let go, take our shoes off, and feel the sand between our toes. That's when we can relax.

There are some people who have been to the beach, but they have never really been there. We can go to the beach and still miss out on the experience. We can miss what it can do for us unless we allow ourselves the time to simply be still and focus on soaking up everything it has to offer.

We don't think about tomorrow. We don't make plans. We don't have someplace else on our minds. We relax into the present, into the moment. The calmness of the ocean helps us become more connected with our inner child. The inner child gets to come out and play, carefree and dreaming, disallowing the adult universe to take over with its responsibilities and stress. For me, "the beach" is any body of water. Your beach could be at a lake, or in the woods on a mountain, or in the desert. It doesn't matter where the physical space is; it's wherever you can find stillness. It can be anywhere in which you are allowed peace and quiet.

If you are not in a space where this is possible, you can always take your shoes off, use your headset to play calming music, slowly sip a glass of water, and sit comfortable, closing your eyes for a few minutes. Sometimes being near a fire offers the same sense of peace. Focus on your breathing and listen to your body. Try to quiet your energy and focus inward.

Assuming you are at the beach, here is exactly what I want you to do:

Be still and really let your thoughts flow; have no agenda. As your energy flows, contemplate these thoughts:

Is your current situation bringing you peace and abundance?

Is your current situation bringing others peace and abundance?

Is your current situation building you wealth, or is it limiting your income potential?

Does your current situation give you the time you want with your family to build memories?

What are your current Beliefs about peace and abundance?

Is your current relationship with your significant other bringing you peace and abundance?

As all these answers come to mind, ask yourself, "Doing what I'm doing right now, with my current situation, where am I going to be in the next five to ten years?"

If that picture looks pretty good, then continue on your journey and know that you are on the right track. But if you find yourself in a place you don't want to be right now, or for the next five years, then it's time to ask your inner child what he/she really wants.

Allow your inner child answer the following question:

If time and money were no object, what would you want to do? What do you really want to do?

Chapter 15

BELIEFS

"What you're believing in the moment creates your suffering or your happiness" – Byron Katie

---

The first part of the BEACH Success System is going to the beach and/or lake, any place that will help you find your stillness, and get answers from your inner child. Now, it's time to take yourself through the second part of the system to explore and help yourself deliver the dreams of your inner child.

The second part of the Beach system is to explore the B.E.A.C.H.

The BEACH Success System stands for Beliefs, Energy, Acceptance, Choices, and Hero.

The first step is to examine and explore our Beliefs. If you look at almost every challenge, every obstacle, every excuse, why people don't have what they truly want, many times it boils down to their fundamental beliefs. Beliefs are our foundation and our guiding compass, navigating us through life.

Think of yourself as a computer and our beliefs the applications. The applications are always running in the background, guiding our decisions. Usually, when we have a challenge with the computer, it is not the fault of the computer but the application. Sometimes we blame the wrong thing when all we need to do is tweak a Belief. We troubleshoot, update, or switch to a better, more appropriate application.

Like the applications running the computer, our Beliefs are running us every second of the day, so our Beliefs can either make us or break us. Beliefs are instilled or influenced in us every day, regardless of whether we know it or not. People say that they know this concept, but that their story is "different." I understand. Our problems can make us feel as though we are the only person in the world experiencing the specific issue.

When we bring awareness and dig deeper into the conflict and challenges we face in life, we often discover that many of our Beliefs actually came from sources outside of ourselves. The Beliefs usually come from a mixture of our parents, family members, religious leaders, government officers, employers, co-workers, and environment. As you are examining your Beliefs, just know that, like applications and software, Beliefs can also be updated and upgraded.

Here is one of my Beliefs which seems applicable to any person adjusting his or her Belief system. When a Belief is serving me by making me feel happy, at peace, and giving me abundance, then I can keep the Belief. Essentially, if the Belief serves me, and it is not harming or hurting anyone else physically, it remains.

When I feel as though a Belief is not serving me, in order to get rid of it, I need to explore where the Belief came from or how it was inherited. I also believe, generally speaking, that Beliefs are not mine or yours, but rather something we've inherited either from others or from our environment. Now that we know that, if they are not useful to us, or are not bringing us peace and abundance, we can give them back to the originator.

Five years ago, I was determined to rid myself of as many limiting Beliefs as possible. I was willing to go above and beyond the call of duty in order to remove them, so I invested literally tens of thousands of dollars to thoroughly investigate and study all of the top materials in the world on the topic of Beliefs. I went to work with Belief coaches and a guru. I still remember as clearly as yesterday, one, when I was done with him, you know what he said to me? "Write down your limiting Beliefs on a sheet of paper, then wad it up and throw it away."

All that money to discover that I can just write them down and decide to let go of them? So, I'm going to save you a lot of time and money! I'm going to show you how to work on your limiting Beliefs. By learning which Beliefs originate with your own self, and which are the result of people outside of yourself, you can edit your Beliefs to serve you efficiently. That's the key- understanding what isn't yours. Uncover your limiting Beliefs by asking yourself these questions:

1. What do you want? What do you really want?
2. What's holding you back from having or being what you really want?
3. How do your current Beliefs relate to what you want?

Now, here's my ritual for getting rid of limiting Beliefs:

1. Write each one down on a piece of paper.
2. Th ank them for helping you this far.
3. Put them in an envelope addressed to God or the Universe.
4. Release them and burn the envelope with a candle or a fire.
5. If you can't burn them immediately, release them with a kiss.

Hold the Belief in your hand, close your eyes, kiss it, and send it away with love. Make sure you make the smoochy sound of a kiss.

My divine inspiration gave me this understanding in a moment of true clarity: We are where we are today - physically, emotionally, spiritually, financially, and with relationships - because of the Beliefs we have, consciously or subconsciously. The right Beliefs will get us closer to our own Inner Peace Outer Abundance.

If you want something - whatever that something is - it will help if you clarify your wish, desire, or dream in order to decide if your current set of Beliefs will take you there. If not, simply dump those limiting Beliefs into the ocean, lighten your load, and head toward your dream. Basically, if you are unable to achieve a goal, you need to get rid of whatever Belief is holding you back.

You can take yourself through my Belief Removing Ritual as many times as you need in order to clear your limiting Beliefs. To this day, I still use this ritual whenever I discover something I want to change.

Here is a list of things you might consider bringing attention to when examining your Beliefs:

1) If you are not happy with your current situation right now
2) If you don't feel your worth
3) If you don't have the peace you desire
4) If you don't have the abundance you want
5) If you feel stuck or trapped
6) If you're in a dead-end relationship
7) If you don't feel you are good enough, pretty enough, smart enough, tall enough, short enough, skinny enough, fat enough, ... not feeling enough
8) If you feel like you are being held back and are limited
9) If you feel as though you are a victim and someone is doing something TO you such as betrayal, lying, being set up, sexual molestation, rape, physical abuse, kidnapping, abandonment by family members and/or lovers, and any others.
10) If you have any negative feelings about anything.... please examine your Beliefs.

There is something in your BELIEFS that is causing you to experience these issues.

Chapter

16 ENERGY

"Everything is energy and that's all there is to it. Match the frequency of the reality you want and you cannot help but get that reality. It can be no other way. This is not philosophy. This is physics." – Albert Einstein

---

The second step of my BEACH Success System is Energy. You must first align your Beliefs with your internal and external values, who you are, and who you want to become. Then harness that Energy to take action and create your Inner Peace Outer Abundance. We each have our own energetic makeup, which is a combination of yin and yang Energy.

Many of us spiritual beings adopt the yin Energy as feminine, receptive, passive, nurturing, introspective, introverted, compassionate, peaceful, soft, and intuitive. Yang Energy is accepted as masculine, giving, aggressive, forceful, self-absorbed, outwardly focused, extroverted, passionate, takes action, loud, and bold.

We each have a combination of these energies within us, but one tends to apply as our core Energy. The key to Inner Peace Outer Abundance is to have a healthy balance of both energies. We need to be familiar with our core and know when to harness each Energy.

The Energy for Inner Peace is stillness, which is yin, and the Energy for

Outer Abundance is action, which is yang. As you can see, we cannot just be in stillness mode without action and expect to experience true peace and abundance.

Whether you are a man or a woman, you contain both energies. You need both to be successful in business, relationships, and especially in life.

One woman I coached was always mild-mannered and said, "I don't know if I have the courage to be an entrepreneur. I'm not an outgoing or aggressive kind of person."

I looked at her and said, "You have a son, right?"

She said, "Yes."

"So, when you were lying on the labor bed at the hospital, did you coax him, saying 'Okay, son, please come out. Please come out right now. Can you please come out? Mommy just doesn't want to push you.' Or did you get on the labor bed and push and push and push until his head popped out? Which one did you do?" I asked.

She said, "I never thought about it like that."

"I know, honey. There's a feminine Energy you use all the time, but there is a time to push and a time to go get it done. If you've been entirely feminine all your life, and don't get your stuff done, you need to harness more of your masculine Energy."

In my life, I use my feminine Energy to connect and build relationships and my masculine Energy to get things done. We need to use both in order to receive the full advantages. Given the situation we are in, we need to harness different energies.

There are both positive and negative energies; neither one is good nor bad. Harnessing it to accomplish your goals requires dealing with the Energy that is coming at you.

It's easy to harness the positive energies, like passion, love, abundance, security, and excitement in order to motivate yourself to take inspired action. When "bad things" happen to us, we can also harness that perceived "negative" Energy felt from being upset, or angry, to help fuel our desires and ambitions to be positive. When dealing with "perceived" negative Energy, I have found a few ways to handle the situation.

The first is to use the "perceived" negative Energy as motivation to make a positive change. For example, when I look at myself in the mirror, I see my waist and immediately begin beating myself up over my diet, lack of exercise, etc. I think to myself, *I shouldn't have had that Thai tea with tapioca!* This "perceived" negative Energy motivates me to hit the gym and resist the urge to "have another one" of those fattening drinks.

The second is to temporarily removing yourself, emotionally and physically, from the situation immediately! Take a few minutes to clear your head and work through your options. For example, the night before the final manuscript of my book was due, I discovered that the wrong copy was being edited. My heart immediately sunk! The hour before, I explained to my children that the book was finished and I would play with them for the next three days. The idea of going back on what I had told my kids was devastating. I felt sick to my stomach. I had to physically, mentally, and emotionally remove myself from the situation in order to keep my ego from influencing my speech and causing me to say something I might regret. I love my editors and didn't want to say anything to hurt them!

In either situation, remove the "perceived" negative Energy as soon as possible.

An incident happened 4-6 weeks before the completion of the manuscript of this book that forced me to apply the concept of removing "perceived" negative Energy completely.

During this period, I truly experienced more and more continuous "perceived' negative Energy that was rooted a year earlier. I didn't honor, nor listen to my own inner child's wishes about the incident. I was in the process of hiring a staff member and the interview went very well. I hired the person.

The moment employment began, I immediately sensed a "perceived' negative Energy. Normally, I would have listened to the voice of my inner child, but this time I did not. There were two reasons why I overlooked the situation. Firstly, this person seemed ideal for the position and there had been challenges filling the role in the past. Secondly, the person convinced me that this "perceived" negative energy would not be an issue and would soon stop.

Like any "perceived" negative Energy, they usually do not go away; they continuously haunt your space. Every time I addressed the issue of this particular energy, the person kept telling me what I wanted to hear. Because this person was ideally suited, I kept buying their excuses and empty promises. I had come to the end of my rope with the situation, and made the decision to completely eliminate the "perceived" negative Energy. Even though this person was exceptional at the job we hired them for, the "perceived" negative energy caused us to release the person from the position.

As I mentioned above, by deciding to accept a "perceived" negative Energy into my life, I made the Choice to extend the situation and let the abuse be part of my life. I paid the price for the Choice, but learned many lessons along the way.

Negative energy creates a space for toxic behaviors, such as whining, blaming, and defending. Blaming others for your situation might not be the right thing to do. In reality, you have the choice in whether or not you allow yourself to live in the mode of a victim. I often hear my clients say things like, "He hit me." "She disrespects me in public." "He is mentally abusive and controlling." "She keeps spending more money". These are repetitive patterns that have not changed in years.

Many people defend their choices and try to justify making wrong decisions; continuing with a job just to pay the bills rather than going for something you would truly enjoy doing is a perfect example. Another common Choice is staying married to an abusive spouse because you have children. Now, I am not advocating divorce; I believe people should stay married and commit to love each other in most cases. But there are some cases where people have come to me and they have been miserable for a long period of time. They live with extreme levels of abuse and cruelty, yet continue to accept this energy in their life.

If you choose to stay, then you have no right to blame others, even the ones you perceive to be abusive. By accepting the "perceived" negative Energy, you are choosing to live in misery and suffering. This is why I suggest people go to the ocean. The calming effect of being near a large body of water cleanses the negative energy and replaces it with peace. Peace is the foundation and building block for creating a life of complete Inner Peace Outer Abundance and making all of your dreams come true.

Once people get fed up in life, they take action and do something different. A lot of people go through life leading a totally average and normal existence. They're not mad, but they're not excited about what they are doing! They are just going through the motions. But when they get angry, or passionate about something, only then can they make a change.

That's the launch pad for change, the starting point for heading in a new direction. So let me ask you these questions, and I really want you to take a moment and think about it.

Is there something in your life that you want but don't have?

How does that make you feel?

Truly, how does it make you feel to not have what you want?

What would it feel like to have it?

What are you willing to do to make it happen?

What kind of energy do you need to harness to make it happen?

Let that very energy fuel your passion!

Chapter 17

Acceptance

"Accept-then act. Whatever the present moment contains, accept it as if you had chosen it. This will miraculously transform your whole life." – Eckhart Tolle

---

The third step in my BEACH Success System is Acceptance. Accept everything: the good, the bad, and the ugly. Whatever hand you are dealt, accept it. Here's why: Acceptance of the negative or positive is the step that will help regenerate positive Energy. When we diffuse the "negative" emotions around a situation, we are set free to move forward toward clarity. When we accept the positive, when our inner child wants something, we have to have the courage to go for it.

The Acceptance step is designed specifically to handle the "negative" energy situations, people, and emotions. We do this by looking for the gift in our current situation, finding gratitude in the lesson, and moving forward.

By accepting others for who they are, what they are, and all they are, we are accepting the same for ourselves. Until we reach that point, we tend to judge ourselves as well as others. Now, yes we accept them for who they are; that does not mean we have to like them or be in the same space with them. We can agree to disagree. I spoke about removing seemingly "perceived" negative Energy earlier. The more you are able to remove yourself from all possible "perceived" negative Energy, the more light and calm you feel.

When we are willing to accept others, and forgive them for all of their seemingly "negative" behavior, we move closer to Inner Peace. Forgiveness is not about the other person, it's actually about you! Here's why: when you forgive others, you consciously cut ties with the negative Energy that is binding you together. I once read that being unforgiving is like drinking poison and expecting the other person to die.

Accepting and forgiving others is more than just a theory! It's been one of the keys to my Inner Peace. What's even more amazing is that acceptance and forgiveness have brought me Outer Abundance as well, which is such a gift!

When you feel angry or upset with someone, that Energy is holding you both captive. If you're not ready to forgive them, at least give yourself permission to accept the situation. Once you have accepted it, you can move on to forgiveness. To take it a step past forgiveness, see if you can send them blessings and good will!

Everything happens for a reason and we must have faith that the reason is positive. Self-Acceptance is key. We have to make peace with where we are in this moment physically, spiritually, mentally, and financially. It means, "Hey, this is what it is right now."

Challenges come up every day and unexpected situations are thrown at us. Whether they be good or bad, we have to face them, deal with them, remove them, and accept them.

When something seemingly "bad" happens to us, regardless of the situation or crisis, we can take ourselves through the Acceptance Ritual.

The Acceptance Ritual

1. Tell yourself, "That's great!"

This should be the first statement when a negative situation arises.

2. Th en ask yourself, "What's great about it?"

(The first reply is often "Nothing!")

3. Ask again, "What could be great about it?"
4. Ask, "What else could be great about it?"

Continue to ask this question until you come up with an answer and a feeling of gratitude.

5. Once you've found a "reason" to feel grateful about the "seemingly impossible situation", you're in total acceptance. At this stage, your mind becomes calm and clear.
6. Once your mind becomes clear and crisp, you can make clear decisions and judgement calls that are good for you long term.

Trust me, I make the mistake of not following my own "Acceptance ritual" sometimes and am still paying the price for it.

It takes time! I've learned that crisis is a must for spiritual development. It must happen for a person to awaken their spirituality, help them grow, and achieve Inner Peace. Acceptance means that we know everything is truly great.

Figure out what's great about it and grow from there. That goes for every challenge; we have to face challenges in order to awaken. Crises and challenges in life are designed for us to grow, to improve, and to thrive.

Often when in the midst of a crisis, we have a hard time answering the questions from the acceptance ritual. I have found that going through the mechanics of asking these questions over and over can help shift my thoughts from negative and blaming to positive and more compassionate. We are also liberated from trying obsessively to find the "correct" answer.

I've coached thousands of people, and people say things like, "What if you lose your leg? What would you say is great about that?"

I will respond: "If I lose my leg? That's great. I'm going to say 'Ouch!' It's going to hurt. But let's put a bandage on it so it won't bleed too much, and the great part is I still have my other leg, and have every part of my body and I am thankful for every one of them. I focus on what I have."

In everything that happens to us, we should always be grateful for what we have. What if we lost all of our money? What's great about it? Let's focus on what we do have: our health, our love, our life. As long as we are breathing, just know that we have a chance to start over and build a solid future.

Remember, it is in times of crisis that we are forced to face our Inner Peace and grow through the challenge.

I had just finished teaching a session on Acceptance and, after the session, a girl left to go home. She got on the highway and into a car accident. She called me and said, "Kim, I'm using your system right now. I have my son in the car, and I don't know what could be great about this accident right now. I don't know."

"Okay," I said. "Stay with me for a minute. What's great about this accident? You tell me what's great about it?"

She said, "I don't know what's great about it right now."

"Obviously, you picked up the phone. What if you didn't pick up the phone, Kathy?"

"Okay, okay, okay. I'm thankful I'm still here. I'm still on the phone, Kim."

"What else is great about it?"

"Oh, my son injured his head a little bit."

"What's great about that?"

"He's still alive?"

"And what's great about that?"

She went on and on, and I stayed on the phone coaching her because she kept coming back to, "I don't see anything great about this right now. My car is broken, and I'm mad," and blah, blah, blah I said, "I don't know the answers for you; you have to tell me." That's what I want to teach people. No matter what happens to you, accept it immediately. Say, "That's great," and then figure out what is great about the situation.

What could you be grateful about in a situation that just happened? I reminded her, "You said you were grateful that you were able to pick up the phone and call me. But let's just say you couldn't pick up the phone and call me. You go to the hospital and you want to know what's great about it. You still made it to the hospital."

Then I told her, "If you couldn't make it to the hospital, or you couldn't pick up the phone, we'd have no conversation, would we? You wouldn't have any kind of pain, would you? You would no longer be here. So what's there to talk about? Nothing.

So as long as you are still breathing, you need to be thankful for the breath that you have. Always. Once you've upgraded to a grateful mentality, you can have, own, or be anything you desire. I'm speaking from experience. I know, because there was a moment in my life when I wasn't sure. As I was on that boat coming over from Vietnam, I was scared when I heard the sharks bumping against the side of the boat. I asked my sister if she heard the sharks hitting and circling around the boat. I remembered how afraid I was thinking that I was going to be eaten by a shark.

My sister said, "No, it's probably wood."

I said, "Are you sure?"

I felt like it was sharks. I mean, over and over and over the wood or sharks were hitting our boat. During those moments I contemplated my death. We were so close to death. We were right at the edge. The captain had just been talking about pirates, then I heard the "pieces of wood" hitting the hull (but I thought they were sharks) all night long.

When you contemplate your death a lot, you grow in character. I know I did. I got chills up my spine. I still feel it now. Just remembering, *Oh, my God. It's going to hurt. I can't swim!* When you are faced with the possibility of your own death, you become stronger. When you arrive at a place where you think you might die, and you think a shark is going to eat you, you think about who's going to get eaten first. And you wonder what you're going to do, what direction you're going to go. *The boat is wood. Is it going to break apart? And if it breaks apart, will we sink? Which direction is away from the sharks?*

As a child, I was sitting there thinking about not knowing how to swim. *I will grab a piece of wood.* I looked around to see what would float; I was looking for plastic. I contemplated how I would escape if the boat did break apart. I'd know exactly what to do. I wasn't just sitting around worrying; I accepted the situation and was making plans for survival. Survival mode. That shaped me a lot. That's why I always say "accept everything".

Like Michael J. Fox said, "Acceptance doesn't mean resignation. It means understanding that something is what it is and there's got to be a way through it".

Chapter 18

Choices

"I choose to make the REST of my life the best of my life" – Louise Hay

---

The fourth step in the BEACH Success System: Choices. No matter what situation you're in, you always have Choices ... Always.

A Choice to be the victim or a Choice to be a victor.

A Choice to be in your current situation or a Choice to change.

A Choice to be rich or a Choice to be poor.

A Choice to be in a dead-end relationship or a Choice to end it.

A Choice to stay in a job you hate or the Choice to find the path that is awaiting you.

A Choice to live your life on your terms or a Choice to buy into the opinions of other people.

A Choice to travel, explore, and grow or a Choice to be stuck in the city that is no longer serving you.

A Choice to treat life as a daring adventure or a Choice to do nothing at all.

A Choice to have Inner Peace Outer Abundance or the Choice to resist.

The good news is that now you have taken yourself through the first three steps of shifting your Beliefs, harnessing the right Energy, and being in Acceptance of everything that comes your way, good or bad. You are now in a great space to make inspired Choices.

Once we are in full alignment with our Beliefs, Energy, and Acceptance, our Choices become clear. We are no longer making Choices based on other's beliefs.

When I had children, I reflected back on my own upbringing to decide how to raise them. I had a choice between discipline through spanking or words, and I chose words. I am who I am today because of the Choices I've made. My parents showed me both extremes of Choice in how to be a parent. As a kid, experiencing so much pain at my father's hand was not fun and I wanted to create a different experience for my own children.

When my son Cash was little, we placed him in a Montessori School for which he had to wake up at 7 in the morning. I suffered that entire year; I hated getting him out of bed so early when he was sleeping peacefully. I remembered how I didn't want to get out of bed that early when I was his age!

After a year of having to go in there and wake him up early for school, I finally said, "Forget it. I'm not going to do this to my child." Now we home school our kids. We have no alarm clocks and we let them sleep as long as necessary in order for them to feel rested.

Most people don't believe they have Choices so they will stick with a job they hate, a person they don't love, a situation they don't think they can get out of, or traditions they don't really believe in but are pressured to follow.

We only have one life and we need to choose to live it in our own way not by the influence of others. Choose Beliefs that fulfill the vision of what you want for yourself. A lot of people don't know that we can choose our own Beliefs, but we have to understand that Beliefs are all - from this moment forward - entirely our own choice!

For example, when I'm staying at a hotel, I still choose to be frugal with the resources. When I leave my hotel room, I turn off the lights, water, and make sure I reuse my towels. I am making a conscious choice to be respectful and grateful to the environment.

I'm not just talking about money; I'm talking about everything. Waste not, want not. If you don't waste things, you will never be wanting things. Do you leave the water running while you brush your teeth? I always turn the water off. It's the little things that count. "How you do anything is how you will do everything," as many mentors of mine have said!

If you are conscious about money and saving electricity, it will show in other parts in your life, and you'll be making better Choices all around. For example, the other day I had an interaction with a man named Joe. He made many seemingly poor Choices along the way to my driveway! He came over and sold me on hiring him as my gardener. Then he called me and said, "I'm going to work on your yard on Saturday," but he chose not to show up. Monday, he texted me and said, "I'm going to be there before noon." Again, he chose not to arrive until 4. When he finally arrived, he said, "I'm sorry. I overslept. I hate my job, and while I was driving to your house, I realized I want to do what you do so I can relax."

That's all he saw. He was telling me, "Kim, I want what you and Robb have. I don't want what I have. How can I quit my job and do what you do?"

I looked at him and I said, "How you do your job today is how you do everything. If you are not successful at the job you have now, you won't be successful at other things."

Joe looked at me with shock on his face and asked, "How is that?"

I answered him, "Because you chose to operate with the mentality of ungratefulness, and when you are ungrateful in life, you are ungrateful with everything around you. Everything, including your job. Tell me, how is it you find yourself working at Walmart as a cashier right now on second shift when you used to be a top policeman? Tell me your situation, I might show you your pattern. So what happened?"

Frank proceeded, "When I was a cop, I hated the hours. I had a female superior and she had it in for me. He complained on and on. "That's why I ended up losing my job,"

When he was finished venting I said, "Until you take responsibility for what you are constantly putting yourself into, you will never get beyond it. It's always going to be somebody else's fault. After he lost his job as a cop, Walmart gave him a job that he did not appreciate.

I told him "You have a job that other people don't have. With where you are right now you should be grateful for what you have. When you tell someone that you will be there on Saturday, you need to be there on Saturday; no ifs, ands, or buts about it. When you say you will be there before noon, you need to be there before noon. How you do anything is how you do everything. Do you see how your actions are continually jeopardizing your words? You chose to not show up on time."

Joe asked, "Can you help me with a business plan?"

I just looked at him. "These past 30 minutes I have been talking to you, and you haven't heard a word I said. Your business starts with you and your word." It was clear to me that he didn't have what he wanted, so I told him, "You don't have any Inner Peace. You don't know who in the world you are, and you don't have any positive Energy. You want all the things that other people have, yet you don't make the kind of Choices that will give you what you want. I'm going to help you, and clear things up, starting with your choice of words. If you say you are going to do something, you better do it. Your mind knows, God and the universe know, but nobody else does."

Inner Peace is about you. You, you, and you. No one else. Your success and failures are all based on you as a person and the Choices you make. Stop blaming others for the poor Choices you made. Start there, and take responsibility for yourself. Remember, in each moment, you can decide to make a new choice, one that brings you closer to making your inner child's wishes and dreams come true.

Chapter 19

Hero

"We are the hero of our own story." – Michael J. Fox

The fifth and last step of the BEACH Success System is the Hero.

Many times, people hope and wait for others to come and rescue them emotionally, physically, and financially. For instance, we've heard "I wish my rich uncle left me some money" "I wish someone just give me a million dollar," "I wish I would win the lottery," "Wish I can marry someone rich she/he can take care of me." And believe me, I thought of them myself in the past, until I found my Hero within.

The Hero's job is to rescue the inner child. Our inner child has been trying to guide us, to fulfill our heart's desires our whole lives, but most people do not listen! Now is the time to rescue our inner child and take guided action. We don't see a super-Hero sitting at home, doing nothing and just talking about saving the world. No! We see Superman or Spider-man or Wonder Woman going out there and doing it! That is a Hero. A Hero is someone who knows what he/she wants and is willing to take the appropriate actions in order to get those things, regardless of circumstances especially when it challenges their limiting Beliefs.

Our inner child may want something badly, but the big grownup in us isn't going to cooperate. To a grownup, the desires of a little child do not seem logical. But the inner child doesn't care! Our inner child may have been wounded so we have to heal that child, love that child, and talk to that child about whatever wounds he or she may have in order to help them heal. If the grownup does not pay attention to their little child, he or she will throw a tantrum.

You must listen to that child, because that child is the voice of the creator inside of our being. Every time we face the "real" world, the child is being buried by Beliefs that are not their own. The Hero has to protect the dream of our inner child and help bring it to life. It will fight the ego and limiting thoughts that are holding us back.

The Hero uses both energies: the masculine Energy to take inspired action, and the feminine Energy to nurture the inner child. For example, we often have thoughts such as, "You're not good enough!" As an innocent child, I wanted to be a Buddhist nun. I saw many Buddhist nuns loving and serving others, and I wanted to do the same.

When I was 8 years old, my great uncle told me stories about Alibaba and the 40 Thieves; he traveled the world and had all these adventures. So I asked my great uncle, "What can I do to be able to go to all these places like Alibaba?"

My great uncle said, "Be a flight attendant; they go everywhere!"

So I thought, "Yes, I'll be a flight attendant!"

Then I told my neighbor that I wanted to be a flight attendant, and she poo-poohed the idea! "Girl, I don't know about you. You have to be very, very pretty to be a flight attendant." My inner child was being shot down and wounded. *Dang, I'm not pretty enough!*

So I went back to my great uncle and said, "I heard you have to be very beautiful to be a flight attendant."

"I don't know the requirements, Little Flower, but I believe you can do anything."

As I grew up, I talked to more people who said flight attendants had to be very pretty and have perfect teeth. I was obsessed with having perfect teeth because, when I was a child, my teeth were far from perfect. I became self-conscious of my teeth. Then I internalized that I wasn't pretty enough to be a flight attendant because of my teeth.

So I started to dream, *God, can you help me to have perfect teeth? Is it possible? My teeth had a cross bite. My dream is to have perfect teeth. Help me, God. I didn't know how it was going to happen; I just prayed. I was obsessed with perfect teeth from when I was a little girl. I even dreamed that I would die and come back as a girl with perfect teeth!*

My Hero always kept this desire alive for me, even when it seemed impossible. The Hero is the keeper of the inner child's dreams. When I got older, and had money, my Hero inspired me to get my teeth fixed, finally! I went to ask for help with the cross bite, and the first dentist diagnosed me with TJM or Temporomandibular Joint Disorder. He said they were going to wire my mouth shut and break my jaw in order to line everything up.

I almost told him to break my jaw! That's how obsessed I was with having perfect teeth. Leaving my dentist's office with the orthodontics referral slip, I went back to my office and talked to my office manager about the referral to Dr. Kemp. She said, "Dr. Kemp is my dentist too. His office is close by and I can make you an appointment."

So I went to see Dr. Kemp. He said, "If you want perfect teeth, it can be done. It's pricey, but it can be done." He had said the magic words, "Can be done!" My Hero was so excited! She was about to deliver my childhood dream of perfect teeth.

"Show me, Dr. Kemp. What do perfect teeth look like?"

Dr. Kemp showed me pictures of some of his patients and I thought to myself, *Oh wow! My teeth were not nearly that bad! He took those people's horrible teeth and made them perfect teeth!* He said he would drill all around my teeth and put veneers on. He wouldn't have to break my jaw after all.

It's funny because, even though I was advised that they would have to break my jaw, I had a strong feeling that it wouldn't be necessary. My intuition was telling me that the process would be easy, and Dr. Kemp confirmed the idea.

He said, "It's very expensive, Mrs. Campbell."

"How much?"

"$1,500 per tooth, and you have 32 teeth."

He didn't know, and I'm glad I didn't tell him, I was willing to pay a million dollars or work for my entire life to get perfect teeth, because this was my childhood dream.

He said, "60 grand" and I said, "When do you want to get started?"

He said, "Next Friday. All day."

Robb wrote him a check for $60,000. He was closed on Fridays, but he brought in the whole team and opened up on a Friday for me and worked on my teeth all day long.

I later appeared on his web site. I was his biggest client, his best case study, and testimonial. I was thrilled to have finally made this dream come true, to have perfect teeth!

Another funny thing about this story is that the Dr. Kemp that fixed my teeth is not the Dr. Kemp that I was originally referred to by the first dentist! Yet another example of how my life has always been divinely guided. The doctor I was referred to was Dr. David Kemp, but the doctor that I was "accidentally" guided to was Dr. Philip Kemp; both worked in the same city. What are the chances?

The moral of this story is that everything happens for a reason. If it feels right and is aligned with my heart's desire, I don't question it. I knew in my heart that they would not have to break my jaw and I was guided to the perfect doctor for my situation. We are all guided, but few of us listen and take action.

What dreams does your inner child have that your Hero is guarding and protecting?

Did you want to sing when you were little?

You tried to sing when you were a teenager, but instead of encouraging you, people around you said, "You're no Justin Timberlake."

So you quit singing? Well, get some lessons! We do that for our children. When Coco said, "Mommy, I want singing lessons!" we took her. She was only 3 1/2. We listened and we did exactly what she asked. That's how we nurture our children's inner child.

Chapter 20

LET IT GO…THE EGO

"The ego is not who you really are. The ego is your social mask it is the role you are playing. Your social mask thrives on approval. It wants control, and it is sustained by power, because it live in fear."
– Deepak Chopra

Our inner child is telling us exactly what we want, but our ego is telling us otherwise. The ego is made up of our limiting Beliefs, scarce mentality, and of all the negative people around us. It's our limited self, so we've got to identify our ego and bring it into alignment with our heart's desires. We do that by asking the inner child, "If time and money were no object, and you could have anything in the world that you wanted, what would it be?" Our Hero's job is to listen for the response and take corrective action.

How do you know if you're living from your ego or your inner child? Here's a test: Ask yourself a question like "Is being a doctor, lawyer, real estate agent, or an Indian chief more important to you than your happiness or your Inner Peace?"

What I have found is that my joy inside isn't just about having the things I desire, but the journey I must go on in order to get the things I desire. For example, when I was in college I was dating Roger. I was a junior, and he was a medical student at Meharry Medical College. The funny thing was, even back then, I was asking the tough questions! One day I asked him,

"Honey, why do you want to be a doctor?" "I want to save lives, help people. That's what we do." He gave me the good response and I was touched.

"That's awesome," I was so happy for him. "Tell me more about it. Why do you love it? What is so awesome about being a doctor?" He then said, "Not to toot my own horn, but when you are a black guy in my family, if you go to college, get through med school, and become a doctor, it will put you at the top of the food chain. As my dad used to say, 'Women love that, and you will have a lots of girlfriends.'"

"So is being a doctor going to make you happy?"

"Sweetie, people have a lot of respect for doctors. So many black men go to jail, or become drug addicts, but instead, I'm in medical school. That's a huge leap for my family and for me."

"Roger, Let me ask you another question, honey. If something happened to you and you no longer could be a doctor, who would you be?" I was just curious and really wanted to know.

"That's not going to happen! Why do you have to ask such a stupid question? And why do you have to be so negative?"

I answered, "I was just wondering, honey. I'm asking because if you put this idea of being a doctor as the ultimate for you, and for some reason you can no longer be a doctor, then I want to know what do you do with that? And who else could you be? And what does that mean to you if you could no longer be one?"

It was just a casual question. I wasn't as deep then as I am now; I was just a curious kid. "Sweet little Kim, just so you know, I will always be the best doctor there is." Being caught up in our ego is when we describe ourselves as what we do rather than who we are at the core, who we are when no one is around us.

In my childhood, I watched my uncle, the pastor, say, "I am a pastor, so I cannot make money. If I were to do business, Kim, I would excel at it, because I am so smart. But because I'm a pastor, I cannot make money." These were my uncle's exact words.

I told him, "Why can't you be a business person and a pastor at the same time?"

He said, "Like I say to you all the time, you can't mix that stuff. You can't."

"But if you are not a pastor anymore, what are you?"

My uncle said, "I will always be the pastor."

Why are people so driven by their Beliefs, the identification to their ego, or identification with what they do for a living? Long ago, when labeling became a process by which we were able to identify one another and communicate, this clinginess to ones ego came to light. This is a bottle. This is a knife. You're a doctor or lawyer. I'm a wife, I'm a husband, I'm a mom, I'm young, I'm old, I'm short, I'm tall.

Labeling in and of itself is not the problem. Labeling becomes a problem when the ego grabs hold of a label and "determines" that it makes you better than, or not as good as someone else.

It becomes a problem when the ego takes a profession like being a doctor, someone who serves mankind, and "determines" that you are "superior" to a nurse. Nurses play a vital role in supporting doctors. In fact, doctors could barely function or even exist without nurses.

Comparing isn't always bad. Hot versus cold is just a comparison without judgment. The unconscious ego uses judgment to make itself feel better, more important than anyone or anything else. That's how you know you're caught up in your ego.

How can you be your own Hero? The Hero is very simple and its main mission is to rescue the inner child. Don't go and try to save the world; the only way to save the world is to save yourself. When the whole world is doing that, everyone is a Hero, and no one needs to be rescued. You are your own Hero, no one else. Don't look for anyone else but you. Help grant the wishes of your inner child, so long as nobody is getting hurt in the process.

Ask yourself, "What is the most selfish thing that you want right now?"

This is a difficult question for most people to answer! Most of my female clients have the hardest time answering this question. For example, I did a women's empowerment program, and the way I teach the Hero part is to say, "Okay, ladies, what is the most selfish thing you think you want? What is the one thing you really want to do but you haven't done it because you consider that is the most selfish thing you could ever do? Give me a list."

One woman shouted out, "I want someone to take my child for a week so I can go somewhere and be pampered all by myself all day long with no crying, no husband, no cooking, no cleaning. I want a whole week of that." Some women would start crying by the end of their statement because they felt so guilty. Maybe you are crying right now at the thought of doing something for yourself. Another woman might say, "I want to be able to have a nanny." Another one might say, "I want to be able to go out, and tell my husband to eat out." Every one of them felt guilty. I told them to just write it down and not judge it. Others would say, "I want to go to the spa, get my hair done, get hair extensions, Botox, I want to go into Bebe and buy an outfit like the stars. I want to go to China. I want to go to Hawaii and just want to travel. I just want to see the world."

I've worked with so many women who are afraid to ask for what their inner child wants and needs. Most men I have worked with don't seem to have a big problem taking care of their inner child's needs. And there is a small group of men that I came to know who were suffering as a result of giving too much power to their inner child.

These men are a ffluent and don't want to mess up their fortune or divorce because it means they'd have to split half of their fortune with their wives. Again, how much is our inner peace worth to us? In my world, when we make Inner Peace Outer Abundance our priority, we become happier and have more Inner Peace Outer Abundance, not less!

When we accept that we have the right to meet our own needs, the right to be "selfish," we have begun the process of creating our own Inner Peace.

For example, most women would never give themselves permission to hire a nanny. For me, I knew that I wanted to have someone help care for my children, and I didn't consider that selfish. I'm crazy in love and obsessed with my children, but I have two nannies taking care of them 24/7 even while I'm at home playing with them myself. I planned my pregnancies very carefully, knowing that I would have to be earning enough income to fund my nannies.

The jobs I have to do for my children consist of love, nurture, hug and kiss them, take them places, spend quality time with them, play with them, and instill Inner Peace Outer Abundance principles in them. The rest, I hand off. Shopping, buying my kids stuff, toys, cooking, and packing things to go on a trip, everything else. The bottom line is, we can have anything we want, we just need to plan for it and take action.

I give women permission to be selfish. At my seminars and retreats, I play the Hero for them to help them awaken their own inner Hero. Once they realize they have a Hero, their Hero will give them permission to be selfish. Look at your inner child. What's the most selfish thing that your inner child really wants? Work on that. That's the Hero's job. The Hero's mission is to create the plan to achieve your inner child's deepest desires. Remember the inner child never wants to hurt anyone; inner child always comes from a place of love.

From what I've learned, we are created in the image of God. Therefore, we are extremely creative. We are powerful, but because of the collective subconsciousness, people are operating below their full potential. The more open we are, the more we can learn. The more we learn, the more we recognize that every one of us is a Hero.

How do we remain open for anything and everything? Travel! Traveling will expand your horizon and ignite you to open up and recognize other cultures, heritages, and history. We will learn the reasoning behind people's actions and develop an understanding, love, and compassion for others and our own cultures and heritage! Our Hero is never in competition with others. Its main mission is to set the inner child free and allowing it to pursue its life-long dream to help you become a fulfilled person that is able to achieve Inner Peace Outer Abundance.

"That's what real love amounts to - letting a person be what he really is. Most people love you for who you pretend to be. To keep their love, you keep pretending -performing. You get to love your pretense. It's true, we're locked in an image, an act - and the sad thing is, people get so used to their image, they grow attached to their masks. They love their chains. They forget all about who they really are. And if you try to remind them, they hate you for it, they feel like you're trying to steal their most precious possession."

– Jim Morrison

Chapter 21

Stress Can Kill You

"The world is a book and those who do not travel read only one page." – St. Augustine

---

As you can see, it's very important to nurture your inner child. With all of the responsibilities of adulthood, such as finding the right job, working, relationship issues, raising children, paying the bills, making sure you get your oil changed, and everything else, our inner child gets locked up and stored away in our heads and hearts. If we aren't careful, it can die there. One of the best ways to bring out the inner child is to go on a trip or vacation.

For me, nothing beats traveling. It's a great way to explore the inner and outer world. You explore the inner world when you open yourself to new places, foods, etc. when you explore the outer world around you. Traveling to new places inspires people and broadens their perspectives. Mark Twain once said, "Travel cures prejudices."

That's why helping people travel to see new places is such a big passion and mission of mine. As an unknown author once said "We must take adventures in order to know where we truly belong." When we open ourselves to visit a new place, we create a bond with the people there, and those we meet personally become our brothers and sisters. In the process, we begin to feel more love and compassion for the whole world, and feel their pain when they experience hardships.

We aren't inclined to jump into fights with people whom we consider friends. We don't fight to kill our family! I believe that our lack of travel and intimate knowledge of other cultures is what contributes to many kinds of problems in the world right now, including war.

For as long as I live, I want to encourage people to travel outside of their comfort zones. I will be lying on my deathbed and still telling someone to take a vacation. I promise that you'll feel better when you take four or five vacations a year.

Many people and companies fail to understand the importance of vacation and travel. Many companies don't support their employees taking a lot of vacations because they think it takes time away from productivity. But studies show that when an employee goes on a vacation, productivity goes up when he or she returns. When you're happy, you perform better!

Ann Price, a friend, mentor, and multi-million dollar entrepreneur in Beverly Hills, encourages and pays for her employees to take at least one 3-week paid vacation a year. It's no wonder that her company was voted the "Best Company to Work for in the World."

Price says "It's impossible to function at maximum productivity without a least a month away. It's wrong to view the benefits as a cost; they're part of what makes us so incredibly productive and successful. This isn't about being nice and pampering employees. It's about creating a business that produces maximum results and changes thinking."

Travel and vacationing are ways of life for me. They are the true path to Inner Peace Outer Abundance. The mission of the Inner Peace Outer Abundance movement is for people to live fully, explore their inner selves and outer world, and create the authentic life of their dreams. When we are on vacation, we are relaxing and that helps with our Inner Peace. When we get back to work, we are more relaxed, creative, and productive, which increases our Outer Abundance, not only for ourselves, but also the companies we work for and those around us.

I noticed that when I get away, at least every four weeks, I am much more productive. Most folks only go away once a year, at best! I ask many of my coaching clients, "When was the last time you took a vacation?" Most would cringe and say, "Ooooh... A looooong time ago."

Eric, one of my good friends, once asked me, "Kim, why do you talk about travel all the time?" I was going to tell him the answer but the truth is that there is just so much to say. There are so many benefits. I just took a deep breath and said, "Eric, just do me a favor and take your wife on a trip. Find out for yourself, then give me a call."

Soon after, he went on a vacation with his wife. During their trip, we spoke on the phone, and with a smile on his face he told me, "Girl, you sure do know what you're talking about!"

One of the problems is that people look at vacations as an expense. It's not. It's a serious medicine for our mental well-being. It's an investment in your personal growth, sanity, restoration, physical body, mental energy, and outlook on life. You can't put a price on that! It puzzles me when people say, "It costs a lot of money to travel." If that is your mindset, please answer these questions for yourself: "How much is my mental well-being worth to me? How much am I worth to me?"

When you go on a good vacation, you feel less stressed and more relaxed. According to the Framingham Heart Study on the benefits from taking vacations, men's heart attack risk is reduced up to 35% (women's by 55%) and women's depression rates are reduced by up to 65%. Stress is the leading cause of illness. Vacation is the number one thing to reduce stress. It's interesting how so many people die of stress-related heart attacks, but still few take vacations seriously. They still see it as a luxury they can't afford, but how much is our life worth to us?

This is a big deal for me because 8 or 9 years ago, Robb was about to be put on high blood pressure medication and we were worried about his health. Despite our busy schedule from running 7 companies, I decided to prioritize our vacations and we went away 3 times in 6 months. The first trip, Robb went kicking and screaming all the way to Hawaii because he didn't think we had time.

But after just 3 days there, he admitted that he needed it. This trip was different because we did not check our phones or computers while we were there. We truly got to fully relax and unwind. He was hooked. After our third trip in 6 months, we had Robb's blood pressure checked and he didn't need to get on the medication after all! This was such a blessing!

It's very simple. The human body is made up of Energy. Exposing ourselves to new experiences and cultures when we go on vacation energizes us. When we relax and unplug, it allows us to access our creativity every time. The Framingham Study reported this: While we're creating these lifelong memories with our loved-ones, while we're exploring the world, everyone comes away refreshed and energized and ready to go back to the task at hand.

So many of my clients are in health and wellness, and they also claim that vacations can help you lose weight. It's a win-win proposition! That's why our company is called, "Live Life Ventures." We're all about living life. We're all about exploring the inner and the outer world. Not just the physical world that we see, but the inner world as well.

So many people live in the "negative zone," or in a "negative environment," and getting away helps them to shift their thinking from negative to positive. When we are on vacation, we are more joyful and can release our negativity, or inner pollution. When we can help reduce the inner pollution, we help reduce the outer pollution as well, because what is in our heads and hearts materializes into our words and actions. When your perception shifts for the better, you change for the better, and your life becomes better.

Any time a person says, "I don't want to go on vacation," I usually want to dig a little deeper. "Why don't you like vacations? There is always a reason why a person doesn't like to travel."

Most often it just boils down to, "I've never been on a good vacation."

Or it can be that their parents told them for years stuff like, we can't go on a vacation because:

We can't afford it.

We don't have the time.

I have to work

Our schedules don't allow it.

Blah, blah, blah

When those children become adults, they think the same way and have the same excuses.

I can't afford it

I don't have the time

I can't take the time off of work

It's dangerous

Blah, blah, blah

The #1 reason why people don't take vacations is because they feel that they can't afford it. The reality is, when you take into account every aspect of what it does, people can't afford NOT to! It's a vicious cycle. My mission: Bring Inner Peace Outer Abundance to the world! People must travel to put more life back into their lives!

When I asked my good friend April, "Why don't you take vacations?" She replied, "I never cared for them." But a few years later she confessed that she never went on vacation because of the guilt she felt because her mother always wanted to go on a vacation. She died never being able to achieve that goal. After 17 years, my friend finally broke that vicious cycle and now takes vacations every few months. She has even gone on to become one of our biggest promoters and leaders of our social travel business.

One of my rules: You must treat yourself to a vacation, regardless of your circumstances. You don't want to deny yourself because you think you can't afford to go. It doesn't have to be expensive. It could be a simple get away. You see, vacations are a great time for dreaming! The next time you go on vacation, you can use the time to listen to the dreams of your inner child. What are your dreams? Have you forgotten about the dreams you had when you were younger?

I am where I am today because of all the amazing trips I have taken in my life starting with that fateful boat ride away from Vietnam. If you don't know what to do with your life and a feel a bit lost, do this NOW. Travel to experience the world and have fun. While you have fun, your soul will tell you what it wants you to do. It will lead you to the next clue, the path that you're supposed to be on!

But what if your dream is to build orphanages in Africa?

Or be able to fund them or spend months at a time helping children in a third world country?

How are you going to do that?

I have the answer for that too!

Chapter 22

Case Study: Bill

"Starting today, I need to forget what's gone. Appreciate what still remains and look forward to what's coming next." --Unknown

---

Now that you've started dreaming, I want to show you how the BEACH Success System can help you to achieve your dreams. The BEACH Success System is a signpost, pointing us to the next step in realizing our dreams. It starts with a scavenger hunt. We are going to find those beliefs that limit us from achieving our dreams. I call them limiting beliefs and they have to go.

The BEACH Success System is a tool that is designed to be used over and over again. It's not just a one-time exercise. It's the antidote to the venom called, I CAN'T.

I have found that, after I have assessed myself and cleared away all of the limiting beliefs that restrict my growth, progress, or love of life, they have a way of taking root somewhere in my life. This world is filled with pain, negativity, sarcasm, and opinions. We see it in the news, in our Facebook news feeds, and hear it in conversations at work or at parties. People put restrictions on themselves and would rather give excuses on why they can't do something instead of giving themselves reasons on why they can.

It's a human quality to receive some of the fears that others omit at times. So, even though a few weeks ago, I cleared all of the limiting beliefs from my life, I find that I need to go over the BEACH Success System over and over again to make sure that they stay gone.

It will take practice, but over time it will come naturally to you. Now, I walk myself through the BEACH automatically any time I hear myself saying "I can't."

Over the years, many people have come to me for coaching and advice. They want to know my secret, my philosophy on how I always look so happy and prosperous. I tell them that I don't just portray myself that way, I live that way! In my opinion, we must focus on having Inner Peace, which leads to Outer Abundance. If not, parts of our lives will always be suffering. What good is it to be happy but in debt and poor? What good is it to be filthy rich but miserable? There is a way to experience life at its fullness.

When should you use the BEACH Success System? Anytime you hear yourself saying "I Can't." I was coaching one of my friends and colleagues, Bill, who is a successful speaker and trainer. He came to me for advice on his marriage.

He said, "I'm so different than most people, there is no way that you can help me with my situation."

I agreed with him, "If you have your mind made up that I can't, then I can't."

He paused for a moment, "But, I need your help."

I said, "Tell me, Bill, more about how you feel about your current situation, emotionally, financially, and spiritually. As I work with you, I will show you that anyone can do this."

Bill said, "Just like many people I know, my marriage is not perfect. The truth is, I haven't been in love with my wife for a long time, and I don't know what to do about it."

I responded, "Well Bill, let's not think of your marriage for a moment. What type of life do you want to live? Who do you want to be? How do you want to feel about yourself?"

It was like pulling teeth to get him to reveal the true motivating factor. He started to talk about his ideal life and the part that struck me the most was that his wife was not mentioned.

"Kim, I just want to be happy, and right now, I'm miserable!" He breathed a heavy sigh and said, "It's my marriage."

"Ok, so now let's focus on your marriage. What do you want to do about it? Do you love her enough to bring her here and talk it out? Can you imagine being with her for the next 100 years? She'll be at your side on your death bed, the person to bury you — could you imagine that?"

"Lord, Kim, 100 years! I don't know if I can take another five or ten years, let alone my whole life!"

"Bill, if you don't do anything, you will be in the same situation for the rest of your life."

"But I really don't think I can go through a divorce."

"Are you sure?"

"Yes, I'm sure. I've thought about it over and over again but…you don't understand Kim, I can't."

"You might be happy to know that the moment you say 'I can't' is when the BEACH Success System starts to work. Tell me, why can't you?"

"I have kids, and all our neighbors and everyone in our life thinks we are happy. If anything happened to our marriage, her parents would die. Her parents have been great to me. They are amazing people who have treated me like a true son, and I can't do that to them. Not only that, but I am a man of God. I had a friend call me with a Christian mentor recently. The call was kind of like an intervention when this mentor found out I was contemplating a divorce. He proceeded to tell me I would be doing un-reversible damage to my family and my children would suffer. Worse off, I would be jeopardizing my salvation and the lineage of my family."

I began to walk him through the BEACH Success System with his situation.

Step 1: Let's examine your Beliefs.

The "B" in the BEACH Success System, stands for: Belief

Basically, you believe that because of your Christian beliefs, you can't get divorced. Now, suppose for a moment that you weren't Christian. What would be the solution that would bring you closer to your ultimate goal and allow you to live out your ideal life?

Bill answered, "The best thing would be to divorce her, live on my own, and live my life!"

"How long have you wanted to end your marriage?" I asked.

"Deep down... Ten, fifteen years."

"So you've known for fifteen years that you should divorce her, but you can't?"

"Right, I can't."

That's where the system really comes in; when you really know the solution you want, and somehow you can't get there.

"Bill, help me understand how your current belief system works, because I believe that if the Beliefs you have right now don't reflect the solution that you want, you need to reflect on your Beliefs. So, you basically want a divorce — that's what you said you want. I don't give the solution; I just give a sign-post that points to your path — you said you want to divorce your wife, but because of your current belief system, because you're Christian, you can't get divorced. No Christian people get divorced, right?"

"Right."

"Do you believe, being a Christian, that you love God?"

"I do, and that is why I don't want to disappoint Him."

"Do you think God wants you to be this unhappy? Do you think you are honoring your wife the way God is asking you to honor your wife — by feeling this way towards her for the past fifteen years? Do you think you've been honoring her, and honoring God? "

He sighed, "No, not really."

"Anytime there is a belief that prevents you from aligning with your inner child's wishes and desires, you need to challenge that belief at a deeper level. You are going to find that it's just a Limiting Belief, and you will see that somebody put it there for another purpose. The problem is that it doesn't work with the solution to your problem. That belief may work for someone else, but does it work for you? Carrying the belief that someone else has put into you — staying with your wife for the next hundred years?"

He jumped out of his seat and shouted, "No S*#T, Kim!" Every time I dragged his situation out another hundred years, it shocked him.

I said, "The limiting part of you, known as the ego, has you operating like a puppet, telling you that you can't do this and you can't do that, and people live their lives operating within those limits. You will drag out the suffering of your inner child because the inner child knows what you want. But for most people, the inner child has been buried for a very long time."

We sat in silence as I saw that he was struggling with what I was telling him. I sensed that for the first time, he was challenging the beliefs that had been a part of him his entire life.

"Bill, I want you to take some time tomorrow with little Bill, your inner child. Go to the beach, be alone, and really sit down and look at what you want out of your situation. Look at what beliefs you hold on to that can be changed. Many beliefs are just a result of your environment and the people around you, they are not organically yours; they are somebody else's beliefs, and they can be changed... instantly.

The moment you can't take it anymore, the moment you are unable to imagine being with your wife for the next five, ten, hundred years, that moment is your moment to shift. Until then, you'll stay stuck. Once you have begun to clear your Limiting Beliefs, your Energy starts to shift from negative to positive, which leads us to step 2."

Step 2: Observe your Energy.

The "E" in the BEACH Success System, stands for: Energy

"So Bill, now that we've discovered your limiting Beliefs, we can move to the next part — the 'E' — the Energy part. Because of your limiting Christian Beliefs, your Energy is negative. You have been feeling trapped, which results in losing your masculine energy.

You are not your full self, not operating to your full capacity. You think you have to play the role of being the male in the family, but you don't want to be there, so your energy is stuck. Your energy is not being directed to the dream your inner child really wants. Now that your Energy has shifted into the positive, it will give us the courage and the power to accept our current situation."

Step 3: Is all about Acceptance.

The "A" in the BEACH Success System, stands for - Acceptance

"Remember Bill, no matter what is happening, we say, 'This is great!'"

Bill was shocked, "What the heck is great about this, Kim? I'm miserable!"

"You're right, Bill. What the heck is great about it?"

Again he protested, "Nothing!"

I said, "Nothing. Cool. What could be great about it? What's been great about your marriage?"

He started to , and after a few minutes he replied, "I love my 3 kids. My wife is a beautiful woman and a good mother."

"Awesome! What else is great about it?"

Bill replied, "We have a nice house. The kids are doing well in school."

I said, "Perfect. Now we can work on your true acceptance."

"It's time to accept and be grateful for where you are and what you have right now, regardless of the situation. Know that everything is great, and happened for a reason. This is where you are right now. You have to accept the situation fully, that you're miserable, that you're not happy, and that you're married. You are currently in a situation that makes you sad.

Take responsibility. Accepting is about taking responsibility. Your wife didn't do this to you, God didn't do it, and your faith didn't do it to you. Thoughts of Acceptance would be: I did it, I made the choice to be with this woman, I need to be responsible right now, at this moment, to take responsibility for the action and choice that I made before. I was one person when I married her, and we have grown apart and can no longer make each other happy.

Now I'm taking responsibility to do something about it, and if I want to be with her for more of my life, then I will stay with her and work to repair our marriage, or I will make the choice to leave. Only when you get to an honest level of Acceptance, can you move onto Step 4 and explore your Choices."

Step 4: Making Choices.

The "C" in the BEACH Success System, stands for: Choices

Know that we ALWAYS have Choices in life, even when we don't feel like we do. We can make Choices to stay stuck or move forward, to be rich or poor, to be happy or sad. The more you follow the BEACH Success System, the more choices you know you have.

"Now is the time to make the choice, Bill. Continue to be with her, and continue to be miserable. Or not. It's entirely up to you. You're the one who must choose to honor your inner child's wishes and desires, and you're the only one who can choose."

The 5th step is where your Hero rises to the occasion and steps in to save the inner child and rescue you.

The "H" in the BEACH Success System, stands for: Hero

The Hero listens to the voice of the inner child, then makes a plan and takes one guided and inspired action at a time to create our desires and realize our dreams.

I suggested to Bill that he take some time and think on the BEACH

Success System. I even suggested that he go to the beach. There's nothing like being in nature like the beach or the woods to reflect on your life. After going to the beach and evaluating every area of his life, Bill and I engaged in weekly coaching sessions.

A funny thing happened during that time. I saw a picture he posted on social media. It was of him and his family, and they were all smiling. He looked happy. Then I saw another post where he wrote that he loved his wife so much and loved his life. I sent him a text that read, "Congratulations, I am so happy that you are so happy!" (I truly am happy when I see that my clients are happy!)

He messaged me back, "Are you f*ing with me?"

I texted back, "No Bill! I saw your pictures online, and your posts saying how happy you are, and when you tell me that you are happy, I believe you. I'm not here to challenge you in any way. I'm here as a friend, and if my friend is happy, then I am happy for them."

He thought things had turned around for him because he decided to be grateful and chose to stay married.

Fast forward a few months when he called me up to say "The BEACH Success System doesn't work all the time."

"Tell me more about that, Bill." I replied with curiosity because I am always open to feedback. There was a long silence.

Then he said, "I need another session. Can we work on it again?"

"Of course, I'm always here for you Bill. However, you don't need another session. You know what to do. We make Choices, and sometimes a choice leads us to feel amazing and other times we feel miserable. Either way, we learn from that choice and it leads us to make another choice. It seems like you are ready to make another choice. But Bill, you already know the drill. You already know what to do. You are just not in pain enough to make the choice your inner child wants."

He said, "I'm not miserable enough to leave her. We have been going out to dinner on dates. We decided to fix things."

"Then stay and keep working on it."

"But don't you want me to leave?" he replied.

"Heck no! It's not my life, I won't choose for you buddy!"

"So when can I leave?"

He was almost asking permission, as if after coaching with me for 6 months, he should be ready to leave. "No, that's not how it works. All I care about is your Inner Peace. Remember step 3, is Acceptance. Accept responsibility for the Choices you made, and accept responsibility for the inner pollution your Choices have created. When you choose to be a great husband and you take responsibility, you say, 'I'm going to be a great husband for my wife right now,' and that inner space of yours makes you feel at peace, then do it."

His voice dropped. "But what if it's not making you happy? What do you do?"

"Listen up, stay there until you are so freaking miserable-— until you can't freaking take it anymore — and then you will make a new choice. Other than that, you're just like a lot of the people who take a picture and put it on Facebook and show how very happy they are. Those pictures are amazing! I love watching people being happy, if they really are happy. Your inner pollution is what you created, no one else."

He tried for a while longer, but at his core, he just didn't love her anymore. For years he had been talking himself into staying, because she was a good mother and she was beautiful. But after a while, his inner child couldn't take it anymore, and his Hero heard that voice and stepped in.

Bill is now divorced. He said, "I wish I could have done it sooner. I've never felt so free and happy. I've never experienced so much Inner Peace".

The Lesson: The sooner you go through the process of taking yourself through the BEACH Success System, the sooner you will experience Inner Peace Outer Abundance!

The key to success is to really dial in to what your inner child wants. Your inner child is the keeper of your true essence, your true desires and dreams. The inner child doesn't care for Armani suits; it just wants to feel loved, honored, and cared for. Inner Peace is a must.

When I watched my children when they were 4 and 6 years old, it confirmed my belief in the inner child because that's exactly who and what they are. They are loving, they have no limits on anything, they have compassion, and passion to play and love and dream and hug and kiss everyone — without exception. They have no judgment toward anyone.

We all have to work on our inner pollution to clean up the space for the inner child to play and thrive. Only once that pollution is cleaned up and everyone has Inner Peace Outer Abundance, only then can we bring more peace to the world. Until that day, hatred and wars will keep happening locally and globally. When we are all living from the space of the inner child, loving, honoring, respecting, and embracing its desires, we are at peace.

I have found that the BEACH Success System is an enlightened way to eradicate the inner pollution that we create within ourselves. For example, my only wish for Bill was for him to be happy. I helped create that possibility, but I wasn't attached to the "how". I was just his guide. I shared with him the tools to use so that when he was ready to make the choice that would make him truly happy, he'd be able to do so.

When I observe myself judging others, I laugh at myself, because I know there is always more inner work to do. I still have to have more compassion for myself and for other people. The more we know about our inner child, the more we become compassionate with others and ourselves. We need to be less judgmental and more compassionate.

Sometimes I catch myself thinking something or doing something "flawed" or "below my standards" — and I think, "Awesome. That means I have to love more, to have more compassion for me." I am a wonderful creature. I am human.

Chapter 23

Secret Wealth Principles

"Before you can transform your wallet from poor to rich, you need to transform your spirit from poor to rich" --Robert Kiyosaki

---

Growing, expanding, discovering, seeking, and developing your inner child is going to take time, and your journey is different than anyone else's. Your journey is going take courage and will be unique because you are a unique human being. Thus, you can't compare or judge yourself or others.

By now, I hope you know how important it is to take care of yourself and your heart's desire so you can have Inner Peace. Again, the journey to Inner Peace Outer Abundance is not a one size fits all. It is different for each individual.

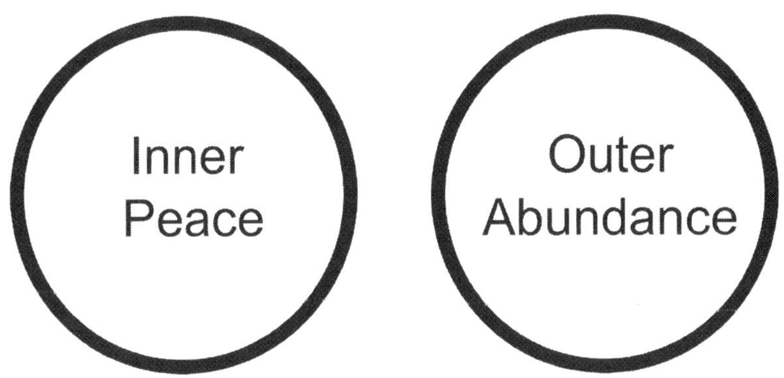

Most people live their lives and either focus or experience just one. But to have a truly joyous fulfilling life you have to connect the flow, Inner Peace with Outer Abundance.

Like an infinity diagram, Inner Peace by itself leads to a life half-lived and is only half of the experience. Inner Peace combined with Outer Abundance leads to a life that overflows with love, joy, peace, gratitude, fulfillment, and abundance. It is the difference between closing your eyes and imaging you are in Bora Bora and having the financial means to hop on a plane and experience Bora Bora for real. It also means to have the financial means to support the orphanages that I love all over the world, building bottle schools in Guatemala, and other local projects while helping others launch their dreams as well.

The opposite occurs when people have the financial means to experience what ever they want, but are still empty on the inside. There are numerous examples of people who have lived and died because they had no inner peace. Many of them turn to drugs; Elvis Presley, Michael Jackson, John Belushi, and Whitney Houston, were all incredibly talented entertainers who Chose to turn to drugs. They were loved by millions of people and they brought so much joy in the lives of the people they touched, yet they could not bring joy to themselves. In their misery, they turned to drugs to medicate themselves to hide their pain.

With some people, it might not be drugs. Some people hide behind a manufactured image or confidence. Some people turn to enhance their outer beauty, with such things as plastic surgery, diets and fitness regiments, and it is never enough. Trust me this is not judgment, I have had a few procedures and I work out and try to eat right. But I loved myself before and I love myself now. These things had no bearing on my self-love and self-worth. I work just as hard on my inside as I do on my outside. Please pay attention and do not ignore any and all feelings of lack or inadequacy, low self-esteem, self-love, or self-worth.

The challenge is for most people, it is easier to live an unauthentic life because it is easier in the short term. It is easier to be in a job you can't stand because even though you hate it, your bills are paid and you are comfortable. It is easy to be in a marriage with someone you are no longer in love with because the pain of separating your marriage is focused on more than the peace and joy you will experience when it is over. The happiness you will feel when you are finally with the person who truly brings an abundance of love to you.

If you don't fit in, there are other people that may also not fit in, and you may fit in with them. Be open to that. The key is do not hold it inside. Know you are beautiful and special the way God made you. You've read about the Inner Peace portion, now we are going to dive into the Outer Abundance part, the financial aspect to living the life of your dreams, on your terms.

Most people confuse abundance with money or a big title at their job. One example is a corporate executive with a VP title and a high paying-salary. But when is the last time he saw his son's school play on a Tuesday? When is the last time he took his spouse on their dream vacation? Abundance is more than just your title or your profession. The ego craves titles and promotions to impress the outside world. The only impressive thing is you have not had a heart attack because of all the stress of working 65 hours a week.

Trust me, I am speaking from experience. Abundance is so much more. It is about time and money. Not just one, but having complete control of both. How much is in your bank account, how much money is coming in… your cash flow, how much money are you investing, what assets do you own and what are they producing, how much quality time do you have in your life to do what you really want to do? Can you decide to take a trip on a Wednesday and leave on a Thursday without asking permission? Can you book a flight to a city one way, stay till you're bored, then book another one way ticket somewhere else? It is a combination of all these things that make up Outer Abundance.

Many are blessed to know their calling early on in life and can follow that path and generate income from that calling. Most of us aren't that lucky.

For me, I knew I didn't want to be trapped in an office from 9-5, especially sitting in an office without a view. Growing up, I did all the right things, just as my family had instructed. I studied while in school, got good grades, a good education, and a good job. Most people are satisfied by earning a living wage and providing for their families. If they're lucky, the can even put their kids through college. However, for me, there's more to it than that. There is more to life than just paying your bills and sending your kids to college.

My husband and I were very fortunate to be able to build 7 companies in the Real Estate profession exceeding a billion dollars in sales in a single year. We worked very diligently building our businesses and expanding till we reached the pinnacle of what most people would call success. Since we did not know what we did not know, we thought we were as successful as we could be. While I was studying ways to be more successful in business, I was introduced to a book that would confirm my beliefs about earning income. The book is called, *Rich Dad Poor Dad,* by Robert Kiyosaki. I encourage you to read it.

The book that really got my attention was Robert Kiyosaki's second book *Cashflow Quadrant, a Guide to Financial Freedom.* In the book, he explains that there are four different ways to produce income, which he put in quadrants. They are the Employee, the Self-Employed, the Business Owner, and the Investor. He wrote this book to help those who are ready to move beyond job security and enter the world of entrepreneurship to create financial freedom that was not taught in college or anywhere else. The first thing to understand is that none of the four quadrants are good or bad. We should all be grateful for what we have.

The first quadrant is the Employee.

Did you know that when a child goes through the educational system the curriculum used to educate our children was designed by the captains of industry at the turn of the 20th century? It was designed by the Vanderbilts and the Rockefellers to provide a basic education so people would be qualified to work in their plants, on their job sites or in their offices. The system was not designed to help you get ahead, but to help you get by and pass. That is why so many people get frustrated when they change jobs and find themselves in the exact same situation.

The average cost of a college education as I write this book is $28,000.00 per year, according to Forbes. These days many people invest a lot of money for a college education and the job that lines up with that degree is not available. If you invest in Graduate school, they train you to be Self-Employed, a higher-wage employee working for yourself.

The big takeaway for employees is to know that your job is designed to provide a living wage. You basically exchange your time for someone else's money. On the surface that looks good. You have a basic set income coming to provide for all your essential living expenses. The downside is most employers sell your time to the marketplace and they charge a retail wage for your services but they pay you a wholesale wage. Think about it, shouldn't your employer be untitled to make money off of what you do? If not why would they hire you?

Depending on the job there may be room for some extras financially but there is always a cost. Typically the cost for a high income W2 position is time. The more you are paid, the more time and commitment your employer expects from you. Many times even when you are not at work physically you are there mentally. This leads to excessive stress and perceived levels of negative energy that you can not escape from because as your income goes up your living expenses go up leaving you trapped and addicted to your paycheck.

Sometimes it affects time with your family missing the dance recital or ball game because you need to get the report done or possibly you are always out of town on business. If the company shuts down or a superior decides to eliminate your position even for personal reasons your income is also eliminated. Sometimes it may be an advance in technology that displaces an employee. Let me give you an example:

In a tiny village the people live very primitive lives. There is a group of 10 men who grab their fishing poles every day and go fishing to provide food for the village. Then one day the village is visited by a leader from a village on the other side of the island; they invented a fishing net which enabled 2 men to catch 2 days' worth of fish every day compared to how many 10 men were catching with the fishing poles. The same output (number of fish being caught) is happening but they are doing it with much less labor. When that happens today it creates layoffs and downsizing.

The employee way of life is the least likely way to achieve Inner Peace Outer Abundance. The moment an employee starts to earn more money, employers find a way for automation or outsourcing to reduce overall costs. Payroll is typically the largest expenses for any business. Be aware a business' first priority is profits and remaining competitive in the marketplace. Think about it, they even have a phrase "Human Capital" to define labor costs. This is also the quadrant that typically generates the lowest income but also the people in this area pay the highest percentage of their income in taxes. I am not saying that to drive fear but to drive awareness. Our minds are designed to do more so if your job becomes obsolete that means a higher calling is preparing you to do something greater. The stress level and uncertainty certainly makes the road to inner peace challenging to achieve.

Think about it. Have you met many wealthy employees? If you have, they rarely have any time to enjoy their wealth. In my case, I was an underwriter for CIGNA making $28,000 a year, but I wanted more. I wanted to earn $100,000 and lucky for me, my boss at CIGNA told me, "It's not going to happen here with your particular job."

If it weren't for him being straight with me, I would never have known. Most people these days will never make $100,000 in a year. I'm not talking about the CEO of Wal-Mart, I'm talking about the normal, average person.

Every person only has 168 hours a week; nobody has any more or any less. As an employee, you are 100% dependent on what you do to generate your income. Meaning if you stop working, you stop earning income. There are only so many hours you can use to exploit the value of your own labor as an employee earning money in a job. Once you recognize that and agree that that's enough for you, that's great because you know being an employee is right for you.

The second quadrant is the Self-Employed

If you say, "I don't like the 9-5 regimen, I want a little bit more flexibility," then the second way is as a self-employed person. This way is the most deceptive way to earn income. Most people confuse self-employed with the third way to earn income, which I'll cover next. It is deceptive because even though you no longer have someone else as a boss, you really don't own a business, you own a job. Meaning, if you are still the plumber turning the wrench, the dentist drilling a cavity, or the realtor with someone in your car every Saturday, the reality is you don't own a business, you own a job. Remember I'm not saying any of these ways are good or bad, I am just giving you the perspective of the differences and which ones lead to Inner Peace Outer Abundance.

There are many amazing, self-employed people out there. When I was working at RE/MAX, I didn't realize it, but I was self-employed. The self-employed quadrant is not good or bad, but regardless of how many self-employed businesses you have, you're still trading time for money.

The difference between employees and people that are self-employed is that employees have no leverage, whereas self-employed people have some leverage. You are also still 100% dependent on what you do to generate income. Typically these people pay the most for their vacations because not only do they have to pay for the cost of their trip, but they also have give up the income they would have earned had they stayed back and not taken time off.

All of those white-collar professions out there, doctor, lawyer, real estate agent, loan officer, accountant, all go through the same exchange of value, which is trading time for dollars. Self-employed professionals typically earn more money per hour, but they still must trade their time for those dollars. Keep in mind that if this is their calling, then they are in the right place for them.

Those two ways of earning income represent 95% of people who make money. But all of those people combined share only 5% of the wealth.

The third quadrant is the Business Owner.

The definition of Big Business is having 500 employees or more. You own a company, people work for you, and that is what it means to have leverage; you are making money off the work of other people working for you. It is estimated that most companies like to earn 10 to 1 from their employees. Meaning, if your total wages including benefits are $100,000.00 per year the company has a goal to earn $1,000,000.00 from the efforts of their employees.

Think about McDonalds, Taco Bell, or Starbucks. The owners of those companies, or in some cases the shareholders, make money by having other people build and sell the hamburgers, tacos, and coffee for them. Burger by burger, latte by latte, they are making money off of other people's work. They have created a scalable business and each employee or part of the team performs his or her role and that success brings profits to the bottom line.

Owning a system like McDonalds, Taco Bell, Starbucks, or a successful network marketing organization like the one that we've built gives a business owner the leverage of having a group of people who create money with you. When we were building our RE/MAX franchises, we were stuck between the Self-Employed and the Business Owner. On one hand, we had some leverage with our employees, but we still had to be at the office almost every day for things to run smoothly.

Some of you may be surprised when you hear this, but one of the best-kept secrets in the Big Business is called the direct sales model, otherwise known as social commerce, a virtual franchise, or network marketing. This is a business model that Donald Trump, Warren Buffet, and Robert Kiyosaki support and recommend today. Because of the costs associated with opening a business, this avenue is available for everyone. They have called it "The industry for people who want to change their lives."

According to world class economist Paul Zane Pilzer, "The real risk is staying with a large organization because your job will probably be permanently dismantled with a few years." If getting hired with a large organization today is risky, the question is, where are the greatest opportunities today? The answer: Become an Entrepreneur. Even for people starting right out of high school, the best opportunities lie in going into business for yourself.

If you want to run a big business, the easiest ways to get trained and get started are either to invest in a franchise or start a network marketing organization. There are other ways to become the owner of a big business, but those two ways are the easiest ways to get into for most people coming from the employee or self-employed way of life. Both models have an existing system and provide excellent training. Most of the training will not be the how to, but training you to think like an entrepreneur. If you want to be an Investor, you have to have capital to invest.

The fourth way to generate income is from the Investor quadrant.

As an investor, you let your money work for you. Warren Buffett, Donald Trump, and George Soros are more well-known investors. People can invest in real estate or businesses. Instead of leveraging the work of other people, they leverage the work of their money. That's right your money can actually work for you. I want to be clear I'm not talking about investments like 401K's or mutual funds. People who invest for a living do not earn income with those types of investments. Those are typically investments for employees and self-employed people. I want you to look at your current income situation and evaluate which way most of your income comes from and where you really want to be?"

The thinking is vastly different in each way to generate income. You can hear it when someone speaks their financial language. An employee wants to know about his salary or wages and what kind of benefits they are going to get. A self-employed person wants to know what is the rate for their billable hours or what their commission percentage is going to be. A business owner will talk about the profit and loss statements and gaining market share. An investor will want to know their rate of return and earnings per share.

Pinpoint which model you are in right now and see if you're okay with that.

Do you like where you are?

If not, are you willing to take some calculated risks?

If the answer is "no," then being an employee is a viable option for you.

If you answer "yes," one option is to look for a good franchise or network marketing company with a product you could see yourself loving for the rest of your life. Pick out one company. Find a company that resonates with you and get a good mentor.

Why? Because you are going to be in an environment where you will find personal development at a fraction of the cost of going to self-help seminars that cost thousands of dollars. Those seminars won't help you nearly as much as the personal growth you will experience while you go through the challenges of building your business! Make a choice. Are you happy being an Employee or Self-Employed? Or do you want a Big Business or to become an Investor?

As I've mentioned above, my husband and I use to own seven companies and we were in the self-employed quadrant, so we barely had time for each other. I still remember during our annual meeting around November,

Robb and I were talking about our exit strategy. We would be talking about how we wanted to get our mortgage company to do 30 Million a month and then sell it or get our REMAX to 500 agents and sell it. We had an exit strategy for all our 7 companies. These companies were simply paying us well but they were not our obsession. We learned a big lesson and like Mark Cuban said, "Don't start a company unless it's an obsession and something you love. If you have an exit strategy, it is not an obsession."

Right now, here are my obsessions:

1st) God

2nd) My family

3rd) Traveling the world

4th) Business

5th) Humanitarian trips

6th) Living, speaking, and spreading the Inner Peace Outer Abundance movement.

Doing what we are doing now, I have seen that when people are taking trips, having fun, working on themselves and working on business to have more financial freedom and time freedom, they get closer and closer to Inner Peace Outer Abundance.

Chapter 24

Bigger Vision for our Life

"Your vision will become clear only when you can look into your own heart. Who looks outside dreams; who looks inside awakes" – Carl Jung

---

All of my life, I have felt that I was meant to do something big. When I was building my real estate team, I started to get a sense of that bigger vision for my life. I was becoming successful and I felt the desire to help others. One day, I ran into a college friend who was struggling to make ends meet. We were glad to see one another and began to catch up. Unfortunately, things hadn't been going well for her. She and her husband were both unemployed, in debt, and struggling to support their two boys. She was really down and out.

I felt compelled to help her get out of her crisis, so I offered to train her and teach her how to be successful in real estate. She jumped at the chance to work with me. I paid for her real estate training classes and all of her start-up expenses, plus paid her a good salary. I really didn't need an assistant, but I felt drawn to help her. Not only did I get her started, I also taught her the ins and outs of how to do work in real estate successfully, which is different than just working in real estate. She was an eager student and was with me for just about every day for the next two years.

She became quite successful and our friendship had blossomed. At least that's what I thought. After two years of learning from me and making a lot of money, she quit. She went to another company and actually took some of my clients with her.

I was heartbroken. We had become good friends and I felt betrayed. In my world, relationships come first, and business comes second, so this was really hard for me. I made a decision not to hire anyone else to help me, that I could run my business by myself.

Six months later, I ran into a high school friend who was in a similar situation. I took a chance and hired and trained her to help me. Within 2 years, the same thing happened! I swore never to hire anyone again!

During that same time, a client of mine came and begged me to hire him. I told him no, but then his father came and begged me. Against my better judgment, I said yes, and this time he lasted 8 months before he quit and moved to another firm.

This happened a total of 5 times! I kept finding people that begged me to help them, but once I trained them and got them up and running, they would leave me. They would promise not to leave, but in the end, they always did. I saw this happen to Robb as well. He helped build many big real estate teams only to have them leave, start their own companies, and become our competition.

We started to realize the insanity of investing time and money into people who would go on to be our competition. This is accepted as normal in the Real Estate profession, but I was not going to deal with it anymore.

What we started to realize is that the real estate business model does not support team building to the level of our big vision. We were in an industry that fosters competition, where there was very little loyalty, and fractured relationships. That was the worse part for me, and it wasn't what we wanted. We were starting to get discouraged in our businesses, even though we were still making good money. Being happy is more than just making money. We didn't know who we could trust anymore. We didn't know what to do.

* * *

Little did we know that we would soon find the ideal business model that would bring our vision to life! In September 2007, we attended another personal growth seminar, where we met a young man who would later become our business partner and mentor. We started chatting and he told us that he was in the travel industry. We love to travel, and we are always curious about business, so we asked him to tell us more about it.

Turns out he was making really good money by building teams of people who worked together AND he got to travel around the world building his business! Ding ding ding! The bell began to ring, the alarm went off! Here was a guy building teams and getting to travel around the world, he was actually living out our two biggest dreams, travel, coaching, and mentoring.

After the seminar, we would keep in touch with him and he would tell us about his travels and his business. We didn't realize it at the time, but we had found the perfect business model for us. In the beginning, we didn't understand what we had stumbled upon, and frankly thought it was too good to be true.

We were still making great money in real estate and mortgage, but we were no longer feeling very inspired.

As fate would have it, in May 2008, the travel company happened to have a training conference in our city. The gentleman we had met previously called to invite us to an event where we would learn how the concept worked.

All I saw was vacation after vacation after vacation. Wow, this could be so much fun! I got really excited about it, and the people around us were very positive. I felt good about that. I listened to my heart, and I liked it.

Here was a concept that actually rewarded you for building a team, coaching and, mentoring, and sticking together! There was a training that weekend about how to launch the idea, and we got invited to attend. We had a big decision to make. We began to have serious conversations about which direction we were going to go, if any. We began to weigh the pros and cons of it all.

Pros for real estate: we were well-established and making great money.

Cons against real estate: we didn't have weekends off. We had meetings all day, back-to-back on most days. We had built teams and, and what we thought were strong friendships with people we made successful, and they stabbed us in the back. It's not their fault, it's very normal in the real estate and mortgage industry!

The conference was coming on the same weekend that I had a meeting scheduled with a person who was going to give us a million dollar listing. However, something didn't feel right to me, something was off. It wasn't that I didn't think I would get the listing, I knew I would. It was a feeling that I was supposed to do something else, something more important. At 9 PM the night before the meeting, I texted my million dollar client and told him something came up for the weekend, and arranged to meet on Monday instead.

We freed up our schedules for the whole two days and went to their training, and thank God we did. We loved what we saw at the training; the technology, the marketing, the concept, the people, the culture. We felt really at home with everything! We met several people at that training who were generating great income every month. We knew if the people we met were succeeding that we could also.

* * *

Before you continue reading, I need to clarify something. My purpose for writing this book is to tell my story and show people the way that was perfect for us. My intention is not for this to be a solicitation. I'm simply sharing my journey and how I was able to find Inner Peace Outer Abundance.

* * *

Travel had me at hello, but I was really intrigued by the idea of a recurring income because it was a foreign concept to me. I was curious and I wanted to know more. What excited me as a people person was that this system builds a team of people. I love people. Since I also love vacations and the beach is the place that soothes my soul, it was like a dream come true that the product was travel-related. Each month, building an income based on passive income, which Robert Kiyosaki recommends, this qualifies as a "B" quadrant business. I thought if I could do this, my income would no longer be dependent on me but the efforts of our team.

Plus, the more success we have together as a team, the more successful we all are. This sounded great to me! I said, "Let's do it, Robb." My next challenge was my husband. Robb had been in Real Estate for 16 years and his identity was not just a successful real estate professional, but one of the top and most successful brokers and owners in the world of real estate. He was really worried about his reputation. He was so concerned about what other people thought of him because he was doing this "little travel deal".

Robb was looking for every reason to NOT get involved in this business. We flew to the company headquarters, met the founder Wayne Nugent, and Robb did his due diligence. After that, he gave me the go-ahead. Within four months, we were making around $2,000 a month. The truth was that I didn't really understand how the money side of the business worked. All I knew was that I needed to build a great team.

I was really excited about this, and mentally I was all in. Robb agreed to support me, though he was very cautious. While I made the shift and this became my focus, Robb thought he would do real estate first and this in his spare time. As Robb's way of supporting me, he joined me as we started to attend the training events the company was doing. Over a two-year period of attending these trainings, Robb started to catch the vision. He saw everyday people who were having success and a shift happened. After leaving one of the events, he finally went back home and put our new business as a priority over real estate.

The reason I tell this story is to exemplify that one's identity is a powerful thing. It was not an overnight process. It took two years for Robb to transform from a real estate guy to someone who has become my business partner and helped us design a life for us and our family.

For the first time in our lives, we were building teams that would stick around! With this model, we all get compensated for sticking together and building our businesses as a team. This was our dream come true!

Chapter 25

The Grind

"It does not matter how slow you go as long as you don't stop." – Confucius

---

Before our new travel business, we were blessed financially. Our businesses required a significant amount of our time, and we never had much time for each other. Since my husband worked so hard, he never made time for his two kids from his previous marriage. I saw all the pain, and I did not want that for us, so we decided not to have any children.

We knew at our current pace and level of responsibilities, we wouldn't have the proper amount of time to nurture a baby and raise children. We were at the office or at appointments constantly, including weekends. There was never a moment off. However, when money started to come in from our travel business, although it was only $2,000 a month in recurring income, I started to think a little differently.

I said, "I think I can do this, and I think we should consider having children." We went on a dream trip, and I got pregnant! We were both excited and very emotional about it. I chose to continue running our mortgage company and building our travel business at the same time, while I was pregnant.

So there I was, running a successful mortgage company, working as a real estate agent, and working our travel business – while pregnant! The single biggest obstacle to building our team was not my pregnancy, nor the demands of the mortgage company or my real estate career – it was me. The biggest problem I had I carried with me everywhere I went. My mind.

As CEO of our mortgage company, I was making all this money from mortgages and real estate, and yet here I am going out after work and meeting with all kinds of people, showing them this plan that costs only a few hundred bucks to join. And lots of people said "no" to me.

Many people said to me, "Kim, you're pregnant. Why are you working so hard on the little travel business when you are already successful and making lots of money in your real estate businesses? You should go home and rest. You must be crazy!"

That's when I came home and cried. I just lost it. I was starting to ask myself, "Were they right?" It was only a few thousand dollars a month, and I knew that I could make a lot more with one transaction in real estate and mortgages. I remembered my partner in the travel business telling me that at first, I would be overworked and underpaid, and eventually it would flip would be underworked and overpaid. I still got really upset and wanted to quit. But I knew that I wasn't doing it for the money, because we surely had the money from our other businesses. I was doing it because in the career I had, I didn't have the time to even think about having a child.

I did it because I knew that once I built my business team I would have the time to do whatever I wanted to do with my children. This was my chance to compress and collapse time. It was my chance to create the freedom part of Outer Abundance.

It was what I saw as my only shot and a shot I was not going to miss. I continued to share the travel business, getting no after no after no and crying and crying and crying many nights. People laughed at me and said, "Kim, go rest, go have your baby, and then do your little side business. Don't waste your time with this stupid travel thing, you need to nurture your baby and take care of your pregnancy." I started to understand the more resistance I was facing, the closer I was coming to realizing what I wanted.

I still found myself wondering, *why do I want this so badly?* I had always wanted to see the world, and I wanted to build something that I loved and that I could do for the rest of my life. I looked around and thought to myself, *if it's not this, then what am I more passionate about?*

I couldn't get passionate about anything else, not even about taking my real estate company to the next level. I wasn't passionate about real estate or mortgages anymore. I was tired of training my competition and having nothing to show for it. I was tired of not having any time to do what I felt I was really here for. I wanted this to work so much! To date, no business in the world had made me cry. This was the first, so I knew it was deep. This business made me cry like a baby. This business forced me to face all my fears and shortcomings at the same time.

My fear of rejection and public speaking was brought to the forefront! Real estate didn't present me with much rejection. I delivered great service, so no one rejected me, and it was different; people came to me. Such a big part of why I did this is because I didn't think I could. Yes, the baby was motivating me, but the biggest motivator was the dreams of my inner child.

If all those other people I was meeting at these company events could achieve their dreams in the travel business, I knew I could too, even if I had doubts or insecurities. I not only wanted to be a leader, I wanted to impact people's lives, and show them that they can have it all. They can have Inner Peace Outer Abundance. I knew this was the ultimate vehicle that could make that happen. For me, failure was not an option.

* * *

We got stuck around that $2,000 a month level for a long time. Because of our limiting Beliefs, we just didn't know how to get past $2,000 a month! I mean, really, does this travel business thing actually work? I can go out and sell a boatload of real estate and make a lot more money this. This cannot be worth it. It's only $2,000 a month.

We literally couldn't imagine going to a higher ranking at all. We kept trying, but we were still stuck. At events, we witnessed average and ordinary people achieving extraordinary results. They were having a ton of success, so what were we missing?

By the 22nd month, we had thought about quitting multiple times. On many occasions, I told Robb, "Honey, all the time we put in for the training and all this stuff, I'm not sure it's worth it." Once in a while, we would get a new spurt of Energy for the business. We aren't quitting. We still like the trips. We still like to go on vacations. We still believe in this.

Things shifted dramatically when we were in Vegas for company training. Now we had been through about 20 trainings by that time, and we knew the content. We had seen it over and over and over again, so we knew the content forwards and backwards. Or so we thought.

What we didn't realize was that our mindset wasn't right. We were sitting in the audience and our team was behind us, and walking across the stage during recognition time was a couple out of a small town in Tennessee. Only about 15,000 people live in that whole town! What inspired me was they were just an average, hard-working couple who had a tremendous desire to chase their dreams! They just hit the level that averages six figures a year. And I'm thinking, "You've got to be kidding me!" But at the same time, I was inspired.

We were irritated and fired up! We weren't mad at them; we were mad at ourselves! We said, "If they can make six figures from a little one-horse town outside of Nashville, we're playing this too small." We went home with a new set of Beliefs and new Energy. Before that change of a mindset, I would buy into the opinions of other people that told me that maybe I needed to relax more and ensure I take care of my body and the baby during my pregnancy. I would let them influence me, and they did not even have the lifestyle I wanted. How crazy is that? Then I heard one of the trainers say, "If you buy someone's opinion, you buy their lifestyle."

Once I started to believe differently, I began to respond to them differently. "I'm doing this for my baby. By the time my child is 5 years old, I'll be retired, traveling around the world with my family, and my children will not have to worry about money for their entire lives. The only thing they will focus on is how they are going to contribute to the society they live in and the world." So I went back, armed with a new belief, a new script, and a new mindset. I still did real estate because it was paying the bills. I started to share the travel business with everyone I met from that moment on, including my real estate clients.

Our business went to the next level when we decided to be 100% transparent and we allowed our mess to become our message. I started telling everyone my new 'why', "Hey you know me and Robb, we ran 7 companies, and on the outside looking in, we have everything. What you don't know is that we don't have time for each other. We weren't even going to have children, but because of this idea, it gave me hope that I would be able to realize the dream of motherhood, which I almost gave up. I want everyone to be able to see the world. I know when people meet people from all over the world, it brings down barriers and the fear people have about other cultures goes away because people see people are just people. You will see me talking about this for the rest of my life and I just want you to see what I'm so passionate about."

I knew this was larger than just a way for me to live my dreams. It was a way for those who want more and have the courage to face all their fears and shortcomings to also be able to have Inner Peace Outer Abundance.

We had been going through the motions, but it was clear we did not actually believe that we could do it. Subconsciously, we had doubted ourselves. Plus our identity was wrapped up as a real estate professional. When we shifted our Beliefs, everything started to change. We saw clearly that this concept could not only work for us, but for anyone else who has the desire and the belief to improve their life.

In five months, from that event where we changed our mindset and made the decision and the choice to win, we hit six figures and we have never looked back. A year later, we decided to sell all seven of our companies and focus exclusively on our travel business. We now have complete time and money freedom and have the type of lifestyle that others said we would never have. Funny thing is, now some of those that said we could never do it are asking us to help them get what we have.

Chapter 26

The Abundant Monk

"Detachment is not that you should own nothing, but nothing should own you." – Ali ibn abi Talib

---

At this point in my story, people usually scratch their heads. They could see how much we thought of the new business model and understood that, if it worked out for us, we would have more freedom, get to travel, and make good money. The part that has them scratching their head is why we would sell each of the 7 successful companies we were running.

The answer is simple: We had never seen a financial model such as this that actually worked! Being the hard workers we are, we liked that you couldn't buy your way to success like most other business models. Here, you have to actually earn it. In order to do so, one must have a combination of humility, passion, determination, communication skills, a willingness to be coached, and ethics – traits that we felt we possessed. But most importantly, you must be willing to face all your fears (rejection, opinions of others), and shortcomings (lack of skill sets and lack of belief in yourself), and do your inner work.

This is exactly the reason why, for us, this concept has helped us put people on a journey to help them achieve Inner Peace Outer Abundance. Many people have asked me, "How did you build your business? My answer surprises them. See, we actually built the business by working on ourselves, by working on our own personal Inner Peace. Our success came about as a by-product of us having the courage to go after our dreams and being at peace with the decision we chose to go.

Some people fail because, after they choose the direction for their careers, they spend valuable time second-guessing their decision.

We don't have time for that.

We put the work in the front end, by finding out everything we could about the company and by discussing it at length.

Once we made the decision, it was all systems go! If more people could understand that they've made their decision and to just get to work, they'd be far better off.

The other part of our success came from partnering with the right people. We poured resources into the people who became a part of our team. Too many companies pour time and energy into other things when the secret is that if you spend that time and energy on the people working with you, they'll take care of everything else!

That was a part of our growth, understanding the need to let others grow and share the vision. Our income, or our Outer Abundance, grew as we grew as people. What I love most about my business is that it forced me to take an inventory of where I am in my life. It made me look at who I am compared to who and where I want to be.

For me, it has been a profound vehicle to learn, grow and face my fears by getting in front of a prospect and having them say "no." Think about it. When someone tells you 'no' to anything, you feel rejected. But rejection is one of the best ways that I have found to learn non-attachment, which is the foundation of my Inner Peace. Buddha teaches that "The root of suffering is attachment".

Srinivas taught the deeper meanings of acceptance and the concept of not being attached to things. In spite of this, he found that his feelings were constantly getting hurt each time someone said they wouldn't accept the opportunity. He had a hard time because he took it personally.

You have to understand that for people like Srinivas and myself, this is way more than a business. It's our life's mission. We truly believe that through this vehicle, people will discover Inner Peace Outer Abundance around the world.

In other words, Inner Peace is achieved by detaching from the 'no's', which, in turn, builds courage and character. The 'yes's' build your Outer Abundance, and give you strength and financial results. I explained to Srinivas that people didn't understand his motives. They thought he was trying to sell them something. I told him that people don't understand our passion and our mission. That it is not just a business to us, it's a spiritual mission and a business venture rolled into one.

Often with business, people can be skeptical and many people make business decisions that are fear-based instead of listening to their intuition. This process was teaching him to accept where people are and not get upset and attached to the outcome.

I coached him, "Inner Peace in business (and in life) means we must learn non-attachment. Now, for the Outer Abundance, you must take inspired action, and let go of the outcome. So let me warn you, it may feel painful, but know that through the pain, you are growing into a wealthy spiritual business mogul!"

The first five people who said, "no" was tough on Srinivas.

"I speak to thousands of people at a time on the campus and they readily agree with my concepts. I've spoken to three people individually and they say no because I'm a monk. It's as if they don't think a monk would know anything about being successful in business."

He was definitely getting frustrated.

I told him, "You have a long way to go, brother, to achieve your Inner Peace Outer Abundance".

I began to coach him. We Skyped every day. I didn't teach him what to say, how to say it, or even who to approach. Everything I taught him was for him. His problem was "between his ears." Srinivas would go on to master his fear of rejection, and now has a team of tens of thousands of members around the world. He's one of the best success stories on our team. He helped us kick start the Inner Peace Outer Abundance movement around the world.

The mistake many people make when they start a business is to think they are going to get lucky. They do not really understand what it takes. They think you won't have to work to make great money. But when you think about the greatest success stories in business (Steve Jobs, Colonel Sanders, Oprah Winfrey) they all had to overcome challenges and grow.

But, the beautiful thing about this business model is that it's purely based on your personal growth and performance. You have to do the work to see the results.

My friend Melina is a great success story, too. She always wanted to be a businesswoman, a mother, and a great wife, but she never could imagine how she'd be able to do it all.

I asked her, "Are you happy right now? What is the one area in your life that you want to change? What is the one thing inside your soul that is crying out for help?"

"Kim, I know I am a good wife. I'm a good stay-at-home mother. But I have not yet become a good businesswoman. I really want to be just like you. I want to be a good mom, I want to be a good wife, and I want to be a good businessperson too."

Once she told me that, I said, "Take it one step at a time. So being a good businessperson will make you feel happy, and give you everything you want? Is that what you want — basically, the Outer Abundance part? Okay then, let's do it. As far as business is concerned, what do you want to build? What kind of businessperson do you want to be? What type of businesses do you like?"

"Oh Kim, I really love helping people, I love to travel, I love to empower people, especially women. I want my business to include all this."

"Okay. So my travel club business and coaching program basically have what you want, correct?"

"Yep, that's exactly right."

"So you see the travel club as a viable business in which you could do well? Do you see yourself in it?"

"Oh, yeah — I want to know how to do it as successfully as you."

I took Melina under my wing and showed her the steps. We sat down and I handed her a proven system for success. I gave her a small goal first, knowing that I gave her a big vision.

"Okay, Melina, you need to understand you will become a successful businesswoman in our concept after you get 1,000 people to tell you 'no'. When are you ready to get started? Give me a date."

She said, "March 1."

When March 1st rolled around she said, "Okay, I'm ready now. I'm ready to go get my thousand 'no's.'" Exactly one year later, on a part-time basis, after she followed my proven system, she was making an average of $2,000 a month and growing her recurring income in her business.

The truth is, many didn't need to go through 1000 no's to get to where they wanted to go. Even I have yet to get through 1000 no's because I'm still on my journey.

Why do I say we need a thousand no's? I have found that when we are willing to go the distance to get to the thousand no's' we have the attitude and the willingness to do what it takes to succeed. We will also encounter a wide variety of obstacles that need to be overcome. It is the overcoming of adversity where people get their power.

When I look at myself today, I know that my accomplishments are the result of hard work, not luck. This was a serious personal effort that Robb and I made, and no one else was responsible for our success. Nothing was handed to us. It was a joint effort between God, our team, and us.

We are so humbled and blessed to be earning our living helping people travel around the world, building memories, serving others through humanitarian trips, and building a dynasty, all by following a simple system.

Now we get to help other people achieve the same. We get to coach our team members to achieve their own Inner Peace Outer Abundance, and that is the most rewarding thing ever!

Since we started, tens of thousands people have joined us from around the world on this journey. We have successfully transitioned from the Self-Employed to the Big Business Quadrant. We have learned through experience that our business is one of the best ways to create Inner Peace Outer Abundance. It's not without it's challenges, but it's the response to the challenges that create our Inner Peace.

Chapter 27

Case Study: Myself

"How would your life be different if... You stopped allowing other people to dilute or poison your day with their words or opinions? Let today be the day... You stand strong in the truth of your beauty and journey through your day without attachment to the validation of others" --Steve Maraboli

---

As you get closer to the end of this book, I want you to remember that the BEACH Success System is designed to be very simple. When you detect in yourself something you want to do but you hear yourself saying, "I can't," that's when it's time for you to use the BEACH Success System. I still use it all the time. I teach it, I live it, and I'm still learning it. In fact, just a little while ago I had to go back to the drawing board myself.

I love to read when I get the chance. With kids in the house, that typically means getting up earlier than them for "me" time. When I read, I like to highlight and underline phrases or sections of the books that speak to me. One particular morning, my daughter crawled on top of me and just laid on me. If you're a parent, you probably know the feeling. As a mother, it's a wonderful feeling. However, I had gotten up earlier than usual that morning specifically to read.

My inner child cried, "I want to read!"

My ego answered, "Too bad. You can't. Not today."

In my mind, the phrase, "I can't" started to repeat itself over and over again. I wondered why I couldn't.

My ego again answered, "I can't because I use highlighters and pens to mark passages that I want to remember. If I don't highlight them, I won't understand the book well enough or remember what I read."

Then I remembered my system: the system kicks in anytime you hear yourself say, "I can't." Tony Robbins says, "When you can't, you must." I don't think I understood that until I had the BEACH Success System. The system starts when you think you can't; you go to the BEACH and do your inner work.

So I pulled out the BEACH Success System and said to myself, Okay Kim, it's time to go back to the BEACH!

My ego said: Kim, don't use the system on me! You can't read right now. You always read with highlighters, this is who you are, so you can't read!

I'm at the BEACH, that's great — what are the Beliefs that make me think I can't read right now?

You believe that you must have a pen and highlighters for you to read. Is that true? But is everyone reading their books with highlighters and pens — is that true, Kim? No, you can still read without highlighters and pens, but you don't do that, that's not you, that's not who you are.

That's great. Just accept it, don't resist it.

But do you really want to read, or do you want to be right? You have Choices. You always have Choices.

I really want to read, I'm going to try to read without highlighters.

I worked on myself, sitting there holding my daughter, to the point where I said,

Do you want to read, or not?

I do, but I really have to have my highlighters!

See? Just like everyone else, I am a work in progress. This is the reason why I have to have even more compassion for myself and other people, because I know my darn system and I still get stuck!

I started coaching myself. *What would you tell your clients if they wanted to read and they needed a highlighter?*

I would tell them "You don't have to have a highlighter to read it. Just give it a try." I would say it nicely... "Just give it a try…"

Lo and behold, I was able to read without highlighters.

The first half of that book is completely underlined and highlighted, and the second half is empty, spotless, no highlights at all! As much as I know the system works, and even though it's my system, I'm still working on it in my own life. I'm sure I'll have another challenge, and one after that to work on. I don't mind. The teacher is always the student. The system and the process is just a signpost.

Eventually the system becomes second nature. I now apply it automatically, and with enough practice, you will too.

Chapter 28

Freedom Found

"The only way to deal with an unfree world is to become so absolutely free that your very existence is an act of rebellion."

– Albert Camus

In April of 2014, our travel company held a convention in Fort Worth, Texas. There were thousands of people in attendance. Robb and I had attained the highest level of achievement in the company, International Marketing Directors, and I was scheduled to deliver a 5-minute speech in front of all those people.

As we were being driven from the airport to our hotel in a stretch limo, I told Robb the story of how when I first moved to the U.S, I used to go and dangle my feet in the pools of the Water Gardens, which was in Fort Worth, and daydream about being successful. When we pulled up to the hotel, my jaw almost hit the floor of the limo. The same Water Gardens, where I daydreamed as a kid, was right across the street from our hotel!

We checked into a suite and I began to pace.

"What's the matter honey?" Robb asked me.

"I'm not sure... I think I'm nervous of speaking in front of all those people tomorrow," I answered.

"You'll be great. You always are," he said, "Besides, you already know what to say, don't you?"

I sighed. "That's just it. I think I know what I want to say but I'm not quite sure exactly which story would be the best."

After a minute, Robb came up with a great idea, "I tell you what, you always tell people to be close to water to find inspiration. Why don't we do the same? Let's go to those Water Gardens I've heard so much about."

As we exited the hotel, we ran into our friend Ed on the sidewalk, who was also part of our club and a brilliant speaker. Prior to speaking, he had acted with Denzel Washington and even speaks on stages for Les Brown. I was honored to be able to share the stage with him. Being that we were friendly with him, after the normal chit-chat, we told him our secret, that we were being awarded the highest level of achievement in the company.

"Hey!" he exclaimed, "I am so happy for you!"

"Thank you. I need to ask a favor of you though," I said.

"Sure."

"I've always loved the way you capture an audience. You truly are an exceptional speaker. Well, I have five minutes tomorrow and I'm not sure what to say. Can you help me?"

"I'll do what I can. What do you have in mind to say?"

We stopped walking. He focused on me and I took a deep breath.

"I'm thinking of saying something about when I was living with my uncle and when I was in high school. I didn't have many friends and we were really poor. I used to go right over there," and pointed to the Water Gardens, "after school and dangle my feet above the water and day-dream. My mind would take me away to a beautiful beach where I was very rich and where everyone respected me and wanted to be with me.

It was right there, just a little ways away from where the convention is going to be, that I, a poor immigrant with bad English, made the decision to change the course of my life."

When I stopped talking I realized that he had a thin smile. "Well, what do you think? Robb says I should say that story, but him being my husband and all, I think he might be partial because he loves me."

Ed asked me a few questions to get the whole picture. Once he was satisfied that he knew what I was going to say, he said there was no doubt in his mind that I should say exactly that. When Ed confirmed to me that my childhood story of all my dreams was an important part of my message, I knew that I was going to say exactly that.

I went on stage the following day and delivered my story in front of thousands of people. The reception to my story was amazing!

Officially, that's when the Inner Peace Outer Abundance movement was born.

People were coming up to me and saying, "I want more Inner Peace and Outer Abundance! That is awesome! Whatever you created, we will promote it! Give us more!"

I had told the crowd that I had struggled with spirituality and money all my life, ever since I was a child. Deep down inside, I knew that my mom and dad were happy with their Inner Peace Outer Abundance. They had spiritual fulfillment and they had their business. They had their work, and yet they still did so much stuff for other people. Why couldn't I live a life like that? When I came to live with my uncle, he planted a belief in me that told me I can't worship God and worship money. I never felt that I was worshipping money. I just knew I wanted more of it.

For many years, I believed he was right, which was why I was torn all the time. I really wanted to be successful, but realized I was holding back because I was afraid money would negatively change me.

With age comes wisdom. One day, I made a realization that changed my life. I figured out that money isn't evil, it only magnifies who we are! Once that became my new belief, I erased the limiting belief, the issue I had struggled with for years that money was bad. I decided to let my inner child take over and she decided to go make the type of money I had always wanted. As I write this, my children are 6 and 5 years old. They may never have to work. You could say that they can retire right now. After 90 plus vacations, to places like Africa, Vietnam, Hong Kong, and Thailand, I am living out the wildest dreams of a poor immigrant kid who would dangle her feet over the water and dared to dream about being so much more.

Chapter 29

Stay Open

"Be open to WHATEVER comes NEXT" – Anonymous

As I reflect back on my journey, I think about what made the biggest difference for me. If you knew me prior to having my children, other than appearance, you would think there were two different people. I'm reminded by Robb of an instance when one of the people who worked for our mortgage company informed me she was pregnant. Instead of feeling any joy for her sharing this wonderful life-changing moment in her life, in my mind, I was saying you are pregnant again? I was so disconnected from anyone having children, not to mention myself having them. So for me to say my absolute greatest joy in life has become my children would astound the people who knew me before my kids.

Just like I said, I would never marry a divorced man with children, one more reminder you have to always stay open to other possibilities. If it was not for them, their love, playfulness, and the joy I see in them every day I would have never realized that we are born with that. My passion for Inner Peace Outer Abundance would have never been discovered. It was when Cash was born that I deeply learned the meaning of compassion. He taught me that we were born to love. We were born with inner peace. Then we are conditioned by the daily demands of making a living, other people's opinions, and our own self-imposed beliefs. This causes the inner peace we are born with to be replaced by fear, doubt, and insecurities.

When we stay open, we can truly expand and stay in touch with our inner child. We are able to really dial in to the inner child's wishes or our heart's deepest desires. When we stay closed, we ignore our deepest wishes and that is where unhappiness comes from. There is a conflict that arises when our heart's deepest desires are blocked by our ego when we feel we can't do something because of what other people will think.

Many times, when people have a desire, even from the deepest part of their hearts, they kill that desire because of their own limiting beliefs. "I love that guy, but I can't be with him because what will people think? I want to do that for a living but I went to school for 4 years and this is all I know." I hear these things all the time. Sometimes these limiting beliefs are hidden or subconscious, possibly someone said something to us and their rules created a fear in us. Our limiting beliefs don't even let us know that a goal is even possible and we shut it down completely.

I was recently talking with a friend of mine. She is an amazing soul and successful in many ways, but she has had her share of bad relationships. She recently met a man with whom she connects deeply, and they care about each other very much. But she has grown kids and does not want to have any more children, and he has yet to meet someone with whom he could have a family. She really cares about this man, but was so shut off to the idea of having children together. She never considered the possibility of adoption or a surrogate mother. She didn't consider having a nanny to do all the things that she was accustomed to doing with her other children that she did not want to do right now. If she had not stayed open, she would have given up completely the possibility of a relationship with a man she may have been searching for her whole life. Not staying open could cost you that one person, that one job, that one moment you have been waiting for your whole life.

When I talk to my coaching clients, I tell them and I'm telling you now, do not worry about how you are going to do something. That is not the important step at all. But you have to follow your heart's true desires. Here is why. The how is structured and organized by limiting beliefs and your why is structured and organized by divine design or your purpose. Let me share how this played out in my own life.

When I was a child, a seed was planted in me. Because I was sexually molested by my relative, I believed there was an increased chance that I would go on to sexually molest someone else. I never let the idea of being a mother blossom. I pushed it away because I never wanted to inflict that kind of pain on any child, much less my own. A normal girl growing up talks about getting married and having kids, but that was not my normal. I would think what if I do something like this to my child? I started to justify why I could not fulfill that wish. I started to think of the pain of child birth, and the idea of getting fat. I stayed busy building my companies; the idea of having kids was completely closed off.

Knowing what I know now, I am grateful for my journey and experiences in life, the perceived good or bad ones. It allowed me to learn so much about myself, which I also see reflected in other people. Because I went through so much pain, I am able to feel and see when people are in pain, just like Rumi said "Go find yourself first so you can also find me."

Now my deepest desires are to spend as much time with Robb, Cash, and Coco as possible. I never had the desire like this before, but I would now do anything to be with them. The way I am obsessed now, you would have thought I always wanted kids. That little seed was buried so deep, I had no idea it was possible. When you stay open, you open yourself up to the possibility of anything and everything that you don't even know.

That is why I always tell people, "You don't know what you don't know." The inner child always knows what it wants. You have to say that to yourself over and over. Just admit to that, and stay open. When you do that, it opens up all the aspects of you coming alive. Sometimes you need to chase the rabbit down the hole to see where it goes.

My greatest accomplishment I have ever had in my life is being a mother to Cash and Coco. They are my biggest trophies. I am sure I do not feel any different than any other mother does about their kids. I get very emotional at the thought that at one time, I was so completely closed off to having them, when they are my greatest blessing and source of inspiration, love, peace, and abundance. If you could just name one thing that defines me as a human being, as a woman, or a coach, it is Cash and Coco. That is where I learned how to really love and have compassion. Because of them, Inner Peace Outer Abundance was born. None of this would have been possible without them and limiting beliefs almost hindered my being open to having them.

I never would have been able to help all of the people I have coached had I not dealt with my own limiting beliefs. I get extremely sentimental, and it brings tears to my eyes just thinking what might have been if I had not been open. I tell people to listen to your inner child. Just a little at a time. Move things from your mind, which is controlled by your ego, to your heart, which is controlled by your inner child. When people want something but they don't know how to get it, they just cut off the possibility. They see what they want as too big of a hill to climb. They cut it o ffand they miss out on how much joy they can have in their life.

Remaining open helped me to complete this book. I wanted to share my message of Inner Peace Outer Abundance, but I hit so many road blocks along the way. We had multiple editors and missed deadlines. I kept believing it could be done, putting in the time and Energy, Accepting the barriers, and making the Choice to finish, finally letting my Hero realize the dream of my own inner child. I stayed open through it all, and here I am- a best-selling author!

In life, if we don't give something we like or want a slight possibility, we do not know what we are denying ourselves and other people. So always stay open and follow your heart and your intuition, because life is full of endless possibilities.

Chapter 30

If I can do it... so can You!

"Instead of giving myself reasons why I can't, I give myself reasons why I can." – Unknown

---

You have read about many of the people I have coached along my journey. The one thing that all these people had in common was nothing happened or changed until they took action. They took the first step to start their journey. So the question is- are you ready to let your hero out? Are you ready to follow the desires of your inner child? Are you ready to take that first step? Because I found the courage, the following things changed in my life:

I fell in love with me when it seemed like no one else would

I learned the English language

I conquered limiting beliefs that were holding me back

I became a highly successful real estate professional

I attracted the man of my dreams in Robb who loves me unconditionally

I have 2 beautiful children

I have a global business that provides for my lifestyle, whether I work or not

I am able to coach and mentor people all over the world

I have the freedom to experience life fully around the world

I am becoming a best-selling author

I am blessed and fortunate to be able to give back and help others. At its richest, this is what life is all about. This is the true meaning of Inner Peace Outer Abundance.

One of my passions now is to visit and support orphanages around the world.

It all goes back to when I was 20 years old when I was unofficially adopted by a sweet and loving American couple, Evelyn and Glen. My dad had passed away, and my mother was in Vietnam, so they became a second family to me. To date, Robb and I, along with our team, have been able to support over 10 orphanages in the last 7 years

We recently went to Guatemala on a Voluntourism trip. I was part of a group that helped build a Bottle School. We did all we could to help a community that, compared to us in the States, basically had nothing. At the building site, together with the teachers, the kids and their parents, and us, we were bending rebar, stuffing trash into plastic bottles, and then we used them to build bottle schools. We played with kids there, and even had to teach them how to wash their hands with soap.

As we stopped for lunch, there were a bunch of kids outside the door, just watching us. Without warning something hit my heart like a sledgehammer. I turned white as my eyes began to well up with tears.

Standing in the doorway, among the group of kids staring at us, was a little girl who caught my attention. Something about the way she looked at me reminded me of when I was in the refugee camp. I remembered the missionaries that would visit and give us food, clothes, and even toys. I had wanted to say hi to them, I had wanted to thank them, but I didn't know a word of English. So I just stared at them, just like that little girl was looking at me.

I told you my life story for a reason.

I was that little girl.

I was once a happy-go-lucky kid that had everything turn against her. I had every reason not to succeed. It seemed as if the world was against me.

I…

was molested.

was raped.

was beaten up by my ex-boyfriend.

was almost killed by my ex-boyfriend.

escaped from war in a communist country.

was almost drowned in the ocean and eaten by sharks.

was almost caught and killed by pirates.

was sent to a foreign country.

was detained and deprived in a refugee camp.

became introverted because I couldn't speak the English language.

almost went to jail for crimes I did not commit.

was sent to live with a family member whose faith meant staying in the status quo.

was told I was not smart enough.

was told I'd never be pretty enough.

was told I was not pure enough.

was told by the world that I didn't deserve to have a good life.

and I almost let all these experiences ruin my life…

BUT… I learned that my past does not equal my future.

I know I have Choices. I can choose to hate or I choose to forgive and to love. There are consequences to these Choices and I choose to seek to understand why people do what they do and that helps me have much deeper love and compassion for me and the people. Because of this understanding, I was able to find peace within me to pursue my heart's deepest desires, which are love, peace and abundance.

I became my own hero and am now living a loving life that is filled with love, joy, peace, and abundance.

All I truly want to convey to you is that: YOU CAN DO IT TOO!

You can be successful and have Inner Peace Outer Abundance. You can go against all odds. I don't care how old you are, where you come from, what you've done, or if you cannot read or write...YOU CAN DO IT TOO!

As you have read in my stories, I could have chosen to give up and no one would judge me for it, but instead, I focused on my heart's desires and I was able to change my destiny and make it to the top of two great industries in this wonderful country.

In this book, I have shared with you the secret to my success. Writing this manuscript has been a healing process for me, and I hope that it helps you heal areas of your life where you are hurting. I hope that my stories inspire you to find your own Hero. Listen to your inner child and have enough courage to find your own Inner Peace Outer Abundance.

Acknowledgements

I want to thank my family, friends, leaders, mentors, and their families:

Ganh Van Ha- I want to thank my father for broadening my humanitarian perspective by instilling in me the spirit of loving, and giving at such a young age. Thank you for loving me unconditionally; your love allowed me to escape to a better life and kept me strong through the process. I'm your baby, and I know that letting me go was your biggest sacrifice. I am saddened that we never saw each other again, but you still live in my heart every day. I have saved up lots of goodies in heaven as you taught me to do. I will carry on and pass on your love to the people. I'm passing on that unconditional love of people to Cash and Coco also. I love you daddy!

En Thi Hong- I want to thank my mother for instilling in me passion and love for people and teaching me to put people first and everything else second. Thank you for teaching me entrepreneurship starting at the age of 6 years old. You were the BEST BUSINESS WOMAN I have ever known; you truly have taught me that when you love and respect people, the treatment and care will be reciprocated. I love and miss you Mom, because you kissed and loved on me so much as a baby. I am now doing the same thing to Cash and Coco. I think I kissed them "too much" but Cash and Coco say "Never enough, Mommy." I trust that they will let me know if I am too obsessed with them, hehehehe.

Also to my Mom and Dad, I wish you could have met Cash and Coco. They would have loved you guys so much. I see characteristics of the two of you in each of them every day.

Robb Campbell- Wow, I'm the luckiest woman alive!!! Honey, thank you for your unconditional love and support. Without you holding on and giving me the space to grow and thrive, I would not be where I am today. You do what most husbands try to do for their wives: love her and give her the freedom to grow into her own independent being to be her own hero. I am my own hero because of you. Words can't describe how much I love you, how much I respect you, and how much I want you more and more every day until eternity. I am giving you the Ultimate Husband Award!!! I love you and thank you for taking care of your three kids: Kim, Cash, and Coco. We love you, Daddy!

Srinivas Bhat- Th ank you Srinivas so much. You are my best friend, mentor, and the most congruent spiritual teacher alive! You are one of the most loving, kind, and pure beings I have ever met on this planet earth. Because of you, I was able to birth the Inner Peace Outer Abundance movement. You represent the ultimate, total Inner Peace Outer Abundance master. You have changed my life profoundly and I can't wait to grow young with you as we continue with our movement. This is only the beginning of the movement; we are barely getting started, Srinivas, and I am so excited about our journey.

Jefferson and Megan Santos- Thank you for being amazing leaders, mentors, and our best friends. Thank you for introducing Robb and I to the travel industry and helping us to create a fun platform in which to launch our Inner Peace Outer Abundance movement. You guys have changed our lives profoundly... not only ours, but our children's, and their children's as well. We love you guys for life! You both are our best friends and we love that our kids are growing up together and traveling the world together. Megan, thank you so much for your love and for being my best friend. I love traveling with you and Jefferson; it is so much fun. No matter where we go, I'm always having a blast with you. I am also so proud of you for pursuing your passion in music; you are an amazing wife and amazing musician!

Wayne & Susan Nugent- Thank you for your vision of progression with the travel industry. You guys are living proof of the ability to master Inner Peace Outer Abundance. Thank you, Wayne, for always reminding us:

"The master in the art of living makes little distinction between his work and his play, his labor and his leisure, his mind and his body, his information and his recreation, his love and his religion. He hardly knows which is which. He simply pursues his vision of excellence at whatever he does, leaving others to decide whether he is working or playing. To him he's always doing both. " (James A. Michener)

John Heerhold- Wow, what can I say? Without you, I probably would still be writing or editing this book. Thank you for seeing the transformational value of this message, the BEACH system that has helped you and countless others, and finally, thank you for pushing me to finish this book and have it published. You are truly a poster child of the Inner Peace Outer Abundance movement. You are like a big brother to me, John. I love you so much.

Matt and Rhonda Morris- Thank you, Matt, for being an amazing friend and mentor and for pushing me to step up and take the mic when I was extremely uncomfortable with public speaking. Thanks to you, now they can't seem to get me off of stages all over the world. Thanks, Rhonda, for your fun and loving energy. It is so much fun hanging out with you and we always have a blast. You are a wonderful wife and an amazing mother. We love traveling with you and your family and are glad that our families are growing together.

Phat and Lan Ha- Thank you for sponsoring and taking care of us when my sister, Kim Golden, and I first arrived in the U.S. in April 1987. Thank you for not only supporting us, but also for financially supporting our families in Vietnam. Thank you Chi Hai for all the love and continuous support of all of us. Without you, many of us would not have been here in the USA at all. Chi Hai, you are one of the most loving human beings I have met! Thank you my beloved nieces and nephews and their families. Thao and Raleigh, Hieu and Hieu, Hien and Hinh, and Jonny Ha. I love you guys. Thank you for taking great care of me so well and made me feel love and welcome when I first came to the country.

Ngoc and Myhong Ha- For raising and loving me when I was in H.S. and College even when you guys barely had anything. Thank you for sharing Christ with me. Thank you for always challenging me to defy the status quo and defy the odds. Thank you for introducing me to my very first personal development book, *How to Win Friends and Influence People,* by Dale Carnegie. Your love and beliefs have helped me define my own and I love you forever, brother! You rock!! Thank you Chi Tu for taking care of the family and working so hard while you were pregnant with Jennifer and raising me at the same time. Thank you Jennifer and Joshua Ha, I love you guys!

Tien Ha and Nhung Lam- (Who live in Vietnam). Thank you for always taking care of Robb and me when we travel to Vietnam. Thank you for running our family restaurant, Bun Nem Nuong Bay Ganh, in Soc Trang, Vietnam, for the past 45 years. I'm so proud of you all. Thank you Thuy, and Matt Rotoni, Vu, and his wife ,Nhu Y and their two beautiful boys. Chi Nam, thank you for always being there, you're one of the nicest beings I've met in my life.

Kim Ha Golden – Thank you for giving me the EXTRA SPOT in the BOAT that night, so I could fulfill my secret dream of being in America. Thank you for taking care of me. You're like a mother to me... you are loving but so tough at the same time. I know I can always count on you... you are always there for me when I need you. Words can't describe how grateful I am for you. I love you! Love my nieces and nephew, Jennifer, Jessica, and Trevor.

Matthew and Janet Ha- For teaching me math; you guys were tough, and I'm glad you were. You set such a high bar and encouraged me to succeed in college, and I did. I love my nephews: Danny, Jason, Vincent, Victor. Chi Bay, thank you for being an amazing sister-in-law to me. Chi Bay, I'm blessed to have you as a sister-in-law, you're like a sister to me.

Tuyen Ha and Hen Duong- Tuyen, you are one of the most powerful business women in Vietnam and take after our mother's successful genes. I am so proud of you. Love my nephews and niece: Ba, Hui, and Khenh. Chi Gai, you're definitely taking after mom's business mind. I'm so blessed to have you as my sister. Thank you for always taking care of me when I'm in Vietnam.

Thanh Ha- I love you, brother, and am grateful to you for bringing me to school and protecting me from the bullies during my very first year in America — you rock! Thank you for being the first sibling to join me in my fun social and business travel club. Brother, Thanh, it is a blessing to have you on this journey with me. Thank you for your love and for your trust.

Elaine and Duane Moore- Thank you to my best friends since college, for your continued love and support. Thank you for protecting me when I was physically abused and almost killed by my ex-boyfriend. Thank you for being there to console, comfort, and guide me throughout the "confused stage" in my life when I questioned my self-worth. After all, you guys were the only two witnesses to the mental and physical abuse I was put through. Elaine, I'm glad you didn't kill my ex-boyfriends who hurt me...when you said you were going to kill them. Thank you for being there for me...I love you guys for life!!!

Erwin and Diana Mendoza- For dreaming together with us. Despite the big businesses we own, we still wanted to do something even bigger...on a global scale. I'm so glad we are doing it now, together. I love you guys like my own siblings. I'm so glad that we and our kids are growing together.

Jessica Nguyen Sholl- Thank you, my loving niece, for running our businesses while we focused on getting my story out to help others. Also, Patrick Sholl, for loving and supporting Jessica during that time. Jessica, you are a leader and a powerful woman. I'm very proud of you.

Marc & Kelly Accetta- For your amazing duplicable system and culture training. Marc, you are one of the best Master Trainers I have ever studied under. You always tell me, "Facts tell, stories sell." I didn't quite understand that at first. I used to wonder, "Why would anyone care about my story?" Thank you, Kelly, you are a powerful mentor of mine, and thank you for encouraging me to share my story to empower women in Kansas City back in July, 2013. That was the first time I publicly shared my story with that many people. I didn't know that my once painful story mattered so much until that day, and I still get notes and love letters from women and their spouses thanking me for sharing my deepest and darkest stories that night. The biggest feedback I got was that my stories gave them much hope to truly go for their dreams.

Jon & Diana McKillip- Thank you for your unconditional love and support, personally and professionally. You both have been amazing leaders and mentors to us. Cash and Coco love you and your family. Cash still talks about how much he loves you and how much fun he had with you on my birthday January 4, 2015. Thank you for your international leadership.

Kyle Lowe- Wow, what can I say about you. You are a love bug. You do have the heart of gold and everyone sees it and they love you for it. When our team speaks of you, they just say, "Awe, we love Kyle."

G Amour AKA Vernice "FlyGirl"- Thank you for encouraging me to get my message out to everyone, girl, I'm doing it now!!! Thanks for paving the way.

Thank You to the initial group of leaders that helped me launch my passion, which is now known as the Inner Peace Outer Abundance movement:

Jay & Ashley Nelson, Vanessa & Daniel Rotoni, April & Mark Consulo, Nadine and Peter Psareas, Kathy & Steve Carter, Joel & Lexi Nixon, Blaine Nelson, Thomas Marchbanks, Allison Ogilvie, Toby Lemley, Ryan Klein ,Melina & Brian O'Connor , Sue & Mike Apple, Melodie Jackson, Nicole and Chad Byrom , Devin and Reina Shelby, Josh Corhern, Rachel Kramer, Marcela Gomez, Drs. Michael and Abigail Donelson, Drs. Victoria and John Webster, Dr. Beverly Hyacinth, Dr. Sherry Baer, Sebrena Sumrah Kelly, Emmanuel Chokuba, Lawrence Taylor Jr, Richmond Ross, Mickey and Blake Duncan, Jamie and Venus Parker, Samantha Johnson, Debbie Townsend and Doug & Rachel Lloyd, Nick & Diane Blase, Helen Psareas, Khoa Nguyen, Tom Phillips, Darlene Martin & Paul Psareas, Marshall Pereira, Bill & Kathy Webb, Todd Payne, Shenna Harris-Gladney, Danielle Livellara, Jackie and Bruce Wechsler.

WOW, WOW, WOW...

Without this following group of early adopters/visionaries/leaders/pioneers, there would be NO Inner Peace Outer Abundance movement. Thank you for the first group of spiritual and business leaders that embraced the Inner Peace Outer Abundance movement. Stephen Lee, Robert & April Sunghee Kim, Paul and Jenny Lee, Jongyoung Lee and Vivian Woo, James and Mina Cho, Susan Lee and Naesin Choi, Jackie You, June & Elizabeth Lee, Young Aea Park, Carita Nyberg, Mikael Karholm, Dr. Jorgen Tranberg and Dr. Raj Vastrad, Richard Kim & Sarah Hwang, Johnny Jung & Joanna Jung, Mark hyoung geun Oh, Seven Jong yun Jang, Jason Seokhun Cho.

Grateful for these friends, leaders, mentors who have made our journey priceless:

Dan & Tracy Stammen, Eddie Head, Janice and Peter Jackson, Klaus Schonewald, Johnny & Crystal Wimbrey, Eric & Casey Allen, James & Maureen Lee, Dennis Bay, Sir Erwin & Ernestina Wang, Don Morton, Raymond and Janie Braun, Ed Blunt, Eric "Happy" Gusevik, Henry Law & Julia Woo, Rainer Zimmermann and Angelika Dahmen, Shelley Blanzy, Jennifer and Rob Flick, Jennifer Loveless, Sarah Thompson, Kristi Walker, Thu Le McLeely, Courtney Tyler, Ty & Christel Apodaca.

Lisa Lockwood, Harvey Walden III, Rock Thomas, Dani Mai, Linda Costillo, Kenn Smith & Nhung Le, Nhu Huong Pham, Julie Vu, Trinh Thuy, Jeff Brown. I also want to say a special thank you to my friend Gwyneth Lloyd for her amazing work to impact all the children around the globe.

Grateful for the founding members of our travel club who made extreme sacrifices getting everything moving. Your vision and persistence made it possible for this movement to begin. Thank you to each of you.

Byron and Susan Schrag, Jeff and Cindy Bolf, Troy and Kathy Brown, Dave Watson, Wes Melcher, Kari & Lisha Schneider, Martin & Jessica Syfko Ruof, Dave and Yvette Ulloa, and Carlos Rogers.

I want to thank one of my best friends and mentors, Clint Arthur and his fabulous wife Ali Savitch, for recognizing the potential of what was inside of me, for getting it out of me, and putting it all in words that everyone can embrace and understand, which has now become part of this book. It has become my message, and my story that will be helping, influencing, and impacting the world. Thank you my Magic Messengers Alumni: Dr. Tamika Anderson, Glenn Bill, Melissa Gordon, Merry Ann Settembrino, Joyce Gioia, Dr. Manjula Raguthu, and Surya Raguthu!

To my editor, Caity Byrne Cba,- Thank you! You rock, you are the best I've ever worked with. Thank you Eliezer Gonzalez, Danielle Livellara, and Hannah Eve Thomas (Even though she has a PC #NoMac LOL) for being part of the cool & fun editing team.

Thank you to my other personal and professional friends who have helped me with my journey in business and in life. I also want to say a special thank you to my Book Launch Project Manager Sandi Masori, "you made this whole book launch process seamless and easy." I would highly recommend her to any and all aspiring authors!

Coach Bill and Marci Pipes, Peter Lopez, Thach Nguyen, Michael Young, Monica Diaz, Frank Del Rio, Roxanne DeBerry, Janet Gresh, Daryl King, Josephine Lennon, Chris Hauck, Tom Aci, Jie Dan, & Ray Nguyen.

Lisa Sassevich, David B Durand, Katrina Sawa, Cindy Powers Proser, AB Masiddo RN, Andrea J Lee, Crystal Gifford, Summer Deaton, Melissa Risdon, Maribel Jimenez, Nikkea Devida, Tonya Davidson, Amethyst Wyldefire, Julio Zolfo, Adele Michal, Kricket Harrison,, Mellisa Hughes, Venus Opal Reese, Scarlit Bloome, Heather Laughter, Eli Davidson, Don Stanley, Linda Blackman, Summer Knight, Annette Daly, Laura Pedro, Bob Burnham, Elton Pride, Beth Banning, Eric Smith, just to name a few. Thank you for helping me birthing the message, selecting the book cover, and picking out the right slogan. I hope I will be of great help for you all now and the future. Love and blessings are sent!

John Mitchell, Nico Michelle Fischer, Diana Henry Cachey, Stephanie Bavaro, Elle Starrett Ingalls, Leo Ruiz, Mike & Sharon McCoy, Dorit Susan Ilani, Mamiko Odegard, Terry & Sinee Schmidt, Lance Lovejoy, Terrence Ng, Nate Bloom, and especially Mr. Robert & Mrs. Daryl Allen, I love you Bob!

Joseph Mccldendon, Gerry McKinney, Anil and Nina Gupta, Afshan and Amin Lakha, Jairek Robbins, Spiro Kafarakis, Kelly Haney, Emile Allen, John Halpin, Michael Wang, Hoan Do, Rocio Partida, Adela Naranjo, Rich Castellano, Lynn Ventura, Dan Ardebili, Gale Ricketts, Kim Snyder, Jean Mueller, Denise Cully, Ron Cully, Kerri O'Conner. Josh Jenkins-Robbins, Lori Taylor, Melanie Coffin, Lisa D Lieberman-Wang, Bjoern Bleiber, Rod & Tiffany Khleif, Graeme Swatton, Enid & GlennTaylor, Brandi Spracklin, Gary Freeman, Suzuyo Fox, Katarzyna Scudamore, Joe Williams, Darren Bouton, Matt Brauning, John Gandara, Kim Snyder, Graham Iles, Jeff Roberti, Joy Curry-Torka, Geri Agee, Loren Slocum Lahav. Danielle and Jonathan Brown, Lana Power, Pa Joof, Brittany Allan, Jack & Susie Porter, Lance Trester, Juan Carlos, Phillip Harvey, Kev Liburn, Jeffrey Tonnesen, Cheryl Parker, Tad and Brenda Schinke, Analia Siele, Andrew & Karen Pancholi, Cindy Broome, and Tony and Sage Robbins. I love you guys and miss you all too, really need a family reunion!

Paul & Melissa Ellis, LaJuan Law, Tobias Rice, Eric Lavender, Khanh Ho, Tiet &Tuyen Tran, Tien Nguyen. Kim Pham & Xuan Tran. Chu Nghia, Anh chi Hai Phuong.

I want to thank my loving mother-in-law, Betty Campbell, for her unconditional love and the outstanding job she did raising her three fine boys. I want to thank my brothers-in-law and sisters-in-law and their families. Jaymes and Audry Campbell and their children, Dean, Laura. Jayson and Christy Campbell, and their children Cambryn & Chloe. Thanks, guys, for listening to my story over and over and encouraging me to share it with the world. I love you guys.

I am so grateful to my AMERICAN PARENTS, Mr. and Mrs. Glenn and Evelyn Clark, for helping and supporting me emotionally, spiritually, and financially, from college to still loving and supporting me to this very day. You both, indeed, are my loving parents. Because you both spiritually "adopted" me, I am forever grateful and now, in honoring you both and my deceased parents, our mission of Inner Peace Outer Abundance Foundation has emotionally, spiritually and financially "adopted" many children all over the world.

I want to thank our pride and joy and the loves of our lives Cash and Coco Campbell. We're totally obsessed with you both. You guys are the love of our lives. You both are our everything. We love you so much that words can't quite describe the obsession and passion for you both.

Cash Campbell, I want to thank YOU. You're only 6 years old, and yet, you are an amazing leader and teacher. You are a Master and you remind me of who I was when I was your age before the world imposed their limited beliefs on me. You are so much fun, smart, and courageous like a cool kid should be. I hope Mommy and Daddy are doing our jobs of not limiting you in any way , and if we are, we give you permission to re-defy your beliefs, choose the beliefs that serve and support you and your dreams. We give you total permission to be YOU. We LOVE YOU for who you are. Thank you Cash for loving on your sister Coco. It reminds me of the way my sisters and brothers, they love on me so much too.

Coco Campbell, I want to thank you, my beautiful and powerful daughter. You're only 5 years old, but you are quite a communicator and a huge love bug. Coco, you teach me so much, especially how to speak my mind and be an authoritative. You have been a commanding and powerful speaker since you started speaking, and have a total sense of who you are at such a tender age. You remind me of me when I was a little girl, always glued to my mother's hip while kissing and hugging on everyone. Like me, you love being surrounded by people. Coco, I am so addicted to you, I can't seem to hold and kiss you and Cash enough.

Finally, I want to thank God, Jesus, Buddha, Universal Intelligence, Higher Power, and my inner child for always loving me, accepting, protecting, and giving me the courage and the freedom to become my own hero. Thanks to my own hero for always diligently pushing my own limits. My hero is amazing; I'm giving her all the credits, for she is masterfully balancing the Inner Peace Outer Abundance of Life! Because of you, the Inner Peace Outer Abundance movement has gravitationally attracted so many spiritual leaders who passionately love to blend spirituality and entrepreneurship together...the way of the future...the balanced way of life!!! Then again, peace and abundance is our birthright!!

Thanks again to everyone who helped me throughout this journey! A special shout out to those who aren't on the acknowledgement list; I promise I didn't forget you, I just couldn't remember how to spell your names. I remember faces, interactions, and I remember your soul and your energy, which is very important to me ... more important than names many times. I love you and thank you! Keep in touch!

Keep in touch!

Website: www.kimhacampbell.com

Linked In: https://www.linkedin.com/in/kimhacampbell

Facebook http://www.facebook.com/kimhacampbellipoa

Instagram https://www.instagram.com/kimhacampbell/ @kimhacampbell

Twitter https://twitter.com/kimhacampbell/ @kimhacampbell

Facebook Inner Peace, Outer Abundance Group https://www.facebook.com/groups/innerpeaceouterabundance